Theatricals

John Watson
Theatricals

For Arthur Dignam, actor

Theatricals
ISBN 978 1 76041 830 4
Copyright © text John Watson 2019

First published 2019 by
GINNINDERRA PRESS
PO Box 3461 Port Adelaide 5015
www.ginninderrapress.com.au

Contents

Theatricals   7

Afterword   139

When certain players acting on the stage
    At Exeter *The Tragicall Account*
    Of Dr Faustus, Conjurer, and as
    A certaine number playing Devels formed
    A circle there while Faustus was employed
    On magic Invocation one of them
    Observed and passed the fact to others there
    That in their circle he had counted one
    Too many Devels. These Devels fearfull as
    To what this strange Event might surely mean
    And each one harkening others in their ears
    Desired the audience to pardon them
    That they could go no further in this course.
    The people also understanding now
    How this thing was each man now hastened out
    To be the first to flee that Theatre's Shades.
    The players too as I have heard it told
    Contrarye to their custom which had been
    To spend the night in reading and in prayer
    Betook them out of towne that very day.

The Irish actor Moody had acquired
    A steady reputation for faux pas.
    When Sheridan chose Moody for the role
    Of Burleigh in *The Critic* – even though the part
    Was small and had no lines – the manager
    Declared that Moody would be sure to make
    Some foolishness and ruin the effect.
    But Sheridan protested such a thing
    Would be impossible. How could he fail?
    Lord Burleigh only has to sit, and then,
    As in the stage directions is made clear,

'Lord Burleigh comes downstage, pauses and while
Near Dangle shakes his head. Then exit, left.'
The actor said he understood the thing
And saw no room for error, none at all.
That night he came downstage. He stared. He paused
And shook his – Dangle's – head, then left the stage.

Poor Mrs Mountford during her last years
Had sadly shown a tendency towards
Derangement; this condition, not perceived
As so outrageous as to require severe
Confinement, she was free within her house.
One day while in a lucid interval
She asked what play was to be played that night
And learned that it was *Hamlet*. In the days
In which she held the stage, Ophelia
Had been her forte, and those memories
Now struck her, and with all that cunning strength
So frequently allied to such insanity
She found the means to elude her keeper's care
And made her way once more to the theatre. There
She hid herself until Ophelia's scene
Of madness. Then she pushed upon the stage
Before the actress who was in that role
And gave so touching a performance as
To startle both the cast and audience
Upon which (it was said) she had used up
Her vital powers and, taken home, soon died.

Once Harold Pinter, as Bassanio
To 'Mac' McMasters' Shylock said, on stage,
'For thy three thousand *buckets* here is six,'
To which McMasters answered quietly,

Affecting emphasis with clarity,
　　　'If every *bucket* in six thousand buckets
　　　Were in six parts and every part a *bucket*
　　　I would not draw them – I would have my bond.'
　　　'I could not continue. Others too
　　　Had turned upstage with me while some walked off
　　　Into the wings. But Mac stood, gravely still,
　　　And like an eagle waited my reply.'

'That Hamlet is the very king – of roles.'
　　　(John Barrymore in 1925)
　　　'It can be played in any way you wish,
　　　While standing, sitting, lying down or, if
　　　You so wish, even kneeling. You can be
　　　Hungover or you can be almost stone-
　　　Cold sober. You can be hungry, overfed
　　　Or just have had a brisk duel with your wife.
　　　It makes no difference as regards your stance
　　　Or mood. There are, you see, a thousand Hamlets
　　　Any one of which may suit your whim.
　　　Why, one night on the stage in London
　　　After I'd been overserved with Scotch
　　　At – never mind her name – I got halfway
　　　Through my *To be or not* soliloquy
　　　When it became at once expedient
　　　To sidle off into the shadowy wings
　　　And heave-ho in the nearest drapery,
　　　After which storm at sea I came back on
　　　To finish off the speech. After the play
　　　A member of the Garrick Club stood drinks
　　　And said, "Why, Barrymore! That was the most
　　　Persuasive and, I must say, daring thing.

I mean of course your pausing in the midst
Of that soliloquy to disappear
From view. May I congratulate you on
Such innovation! You seemed quite distraught
And yet the thing was startling!" "Yes," I said,
"I felt a little overcome myself."'

Mrs Siddons spoke disparagingly
Of dour and stubborn Scottish audiences.
'I'm used to speak to animated clay
But there I find I must melt obdurate stone.
At last I thought to make one final try
And if this could not touch the Scots, I vowed
To cross the Tweed no more.' And so she stressed
And coiled her powers to the ultimate
And in one passage reached pure emphasis.
She knew that she could do no more. She paused.
She waited as the lasting silence spread
And washed and settled, broken by one voice
Remarking, 'That's no' bad!' This ludicrous
And parsimonious praise was so absurd
The audience was convulsed with laughter then
Which soon was followed by tumultuous waves
Of such applause as made her feel at once
This Scottish audience could do no wrong.

A gangling youth with face as pale as ash
Stood in the wings, wide-eyed with fear, and said,
'I don't think I can keep on doing this.
That Mrs Siddons – how she looks at you!'
Cast as a steward whom the Queen rebukes
He trembled still. 'That Mrs Siddons plays
As if the thing were earnest! How she glares

And looks me through and through with those black eyes.
I would not for the world meet her again
On stage, and have to admit my fault once more.'

When Mrs Siddons made her stage farewell
    At Covent Garden in *Macbeth* the crowds
    Had gathered from an early hour, and when
    The doors were opened every seat was filled
    And people stood and hung from every point.
    Then, at 'the perfumes of Arabia',
    The hush became so palpable that soon
    It must burst frothing like a flood.
    And at her final line the applause became
    Ungovernable. They stood on benches, and,
    Demanding that the play be not allowed
    To pass this scene, kept up such long applause
    That Chapman (who should rightly still confront
    The ghost of Banquo and resolve those crimes
    By paying with his life for Duncan's death)
    Came forward and at last quelling the crowd
    Agreed that if this were their ardent wish
    The play should not proceed beyond that point.

John Baldwin Buckstone of the Theatre Royal
    As manager was somewhat cavalier
    In his respect for new and untried plays.
    His office was the final resting place
    For countless manuscripts solicited
    And unsolicited, lost to the world.
    One author came indignantly to claim
    His five-act play in manuscript, once sent,
    Never returned. Buckstone was genial.
    'I'm sorry that your play cannot be found

But go upstairs to my office. There you'll see
A lot of three-act plays and, mixed with them,
A lot of two-act plays. Take one of each.'

His failed *Macbeth* had closed. Ralph Richardson
Approached a fellow actor in the street.
'Give me five pounds.' A pause. 'Give me five pounds.
And if you don't I'll have it put about
That you were in the cast of my *Macbeth*.'

Sir Peter Hall admiring of his friend:
'A lovely day. *The Cherry Orchard*. Ralph
Rehearsing Firs by walking through the scene:
"So now I come in slippers through the door.
Good heavens, there's nobody here. Good Lord,
They've all gone. Now I walk across the room.
I look out. Can't see anything. I go
Towards the sofa feeling very tired.
I sit down, drop my stick, too tired now
To take it up. I lie back, and I want
To put my legs up, but I can't. Then I die."'

'Ralph had to take a silver tray on stage
And set it down and leave with some remark.
As I was waiting in the wings, he came
Yet seemed tonight concerned about the tray:
"Oh! Oh! Oh! Celia Bannerman
Has eaten a biscuit! Oh! The pattern's gone."'

To see Cordelia corpsing was as strange
As seeing Garrick laughing in the role
Of grieving Lear. Yet all of this and more
Occurred one summer night at Drury Lane.

An actor 'corpses' when, while lying 'dead',
He's seen by members of the audience
To rock with laughter. Cordelia did
When Lear and all the nobles of the court
In mourning dead Cordelia, saw in the pit,
An apparition leaning at the rails.
A butcher on the first bench of the pit
Accustomed as he was habitually
To be accompanied by his mastiff dog
Had brought that creature to the theatre, where
Because the heat was overpowering there,
He had removed his powdered Sunday wig
And placed it, absent-mindedly perhaps,
Upon that quadruped which leaned its paws
Sagacious as a critic, head upturned,
Against the railing, close below the stage.
Thus Garrick at that moment when he mourns
The daughter he has lowered to the boards,
And mind frays like a sailing cloth in wind,
Saw in the gloom this mastiff in its wig
Attentive, salivating at the scene.
So, in an unexpected turn,
Cordelia, Lear and all the gathered court
Ran laughing from the stage into the wings.

A lady came to Garrick's dressing room
    Bearing a message as mysterious
As it was promising. There was, she said,
A beautiful and rich young woman who,
On seeing him act as Lothario
Had lost her heart and longed to marry him.
The lady begged to ask might she convey

To her petitioner some word of hope?
And he replied that it would be an honour
To wait upon her. So that lady said
She would arrange a meeting and return
Within the week. But several months had passed
Before he met the lady in the street
By chance. He asked about the meeting. 'Ah!'
The lady said. 'She finds her feelings changed.
At Drury Lane she saw you once again –
As Abel Drugger in *The Alchemist*.'

When Mrs Cross (who formerly had played
    At Covent Garden) travelled to the north
To act in Glasgow, something strange occurred.
A magistrate was in the audience
As Mrs Cross began her entrance. 'Stop!'
The magistrate leapt up and shouted, 'Stop
The play! I must speak to that lady.' So
Imperative, so urgent seemed this plea,
The theatre manager appeared at once
And closed the curtain. In her dressing room
The magistrate met Mrs Cross *once more*!
After a restive, puzzled interval
The manager addressed the audience
And told them how this matter lay. This was,
He said, a tale quite as remarkable
As any play this management had shown
(Or even this, the interrupted play
Which soon he hoped would happily be resumed):
The magistrate and Mrs Cross had found,
Much to their startled, mutual delight
That twenty years before this fateful night

They had been married, and, through Circumstance,
As fickle as might ever be devised
By any dramatist, had been by Fate
Parted, while each believed the other perished.
After the play (which happily he hoped
Might soon resume) he wished the audience
Should (with the indulgence of the principals
In this Reverse of Fortune) celebrate
With all the cast this strange denouement.

At dinner there was talk of Sheridan.
Comparison was made between the stage –
The humour of *The Critic* – and those jests
For which he is well known, the *critical*
Discernible in all his stratagems
Such as his jest at Richardson's expense.
The author being out by hackney coach
Beguiling pleasantly the afternoon
Saw Richardson. He slowed and asked him in
To share the coach. Almost at once he raised
A topic on which Richardson (who was
The very soul of disputatiousness)
Was sure to disagree with him. And soon,
Affecting to be mortified at this,
He said, 'I cannot bear this argument.
I'll not stay longer in this coach with you,'
And so stepped down and left him in some haste.
From the departing coach door, Richardson
Hallooed in triumph, 'Ah! You're beat! You're beat!'
Nor was it until later, when the heat
Of victory had cooled, that Richardson
Found he must pay the five hours' hackney fare.

The praise of Shakespeare being everywhere
    So universal, it is pleasing still
    To find a fresh criterion. So here,
    A French enthusiast writes glowingly
    Of Shakespeare's apt particularity
    Of detail, singling out his reference to
    The Scottish climate in the following words:
    'Hail, hail, all hail!' '*Grêle, grêle, toute grêle!*'

This incident refers to Barrington,
    Pickpocket, author, transportee,
    Who wrote the following familiar lines:
    'True patriots we, for be it understood
    We left our country for our country's good',
    Which lines are from the prologue to his play
    Performed by convict troupes in Sydney Town.
    A gentleman was in the pit one night;
    The actors on the stage were indistinct
    So boisterously crowded was the audience.
    This gentleman, discovering his watch
    No longer on his person, turned. Nearby
    Stood Barrington whom he accused at once
    Of stealing it. And Barrington, in a fright,
    Gave up a watch to him without a word.
    And now the play engaged that gentleman
    Until, returning home, he found his watch
    Still on the table, and he saw that he
    Robbed Barrington of someone else's watch.

Of inadvertent humour on the stage;
    Of accident or mischievous intent
    Amongst the players; of misplaced syllables
    And consonants reversed: In 1810,

For instance, several times (to give
A trivial incident) one actor said,
'How sharper than a serpent's *thanks* it is
To have a *toothless* child.' Another too

('Old Parker') used to say, so frequently,
'Take then this coisoned pup' that when, for once,
He got it right the audience said, 'No, No.'
And bade him say it as they'd come to hear.

Another was to be relied upon
To say, not 'Stand and let the coffin pass'
But always, 'Stand and let the parson cough',
And he too had a loyal following.

To these might well be added instances
Of interruptions of another kind
Exemplified in Kemble's sudden pause
When acting in a country hall in which

A child was crying ceaselessly. He glared.
'Stop! Stop the play! Unless the play be stopped
This child cannot with ease cry on.' This trope
Has several variants and parallels,

Including Ethel Barrymore's request
To an audience that they might speak up because,
While she could hear all they were saying
With the utmost clarity, she feared she must

Point out her colleague, Mr Cherry, was
A little hard of hearing. Not far off
From such resourcefulness, lies that caprice
Which makes one actor try to discompose

Another. Instances are legion. One
May here suffice. It is of Beerbohm Tree,
As Mephistopheles to Ainley's Faust.
By testing Faust in unexpected ways

He sought to test the other actor's skills,
By offering gratuitous challenges,
Contriving that the wooden cup, which Faust
Must use, be screwed down to the table top.

A second instance clamours for its share
Of limelight: in a New York *Salome*,
The stage hands in that air of merriment
Which final nights may often generate

Sent on, instead of John the Baptist's head
Beneath the gruesome cloth, for Salome
In exultation to disclose,
A heaped up platter of ham sandwiches.

Towards the end of Congreve's *Love for Love*,
    The scene required the entire company
    To speak. The ricochet of repartee
    Crisscrossed like searchlights in the wartime sky,
    Then stopped quite suddenly. Instead
    The silence of a blackout stirred and hung.
    This awkwardness was broken only by
    The prompter's piercing whisper. No one spoke.
    And still that shifting silence held the stage.
    No one could speak. The prompter raised his voice.
    And then Dame Edith Evans in that tone
    Which once immortalised '*A handbag?*' and
    Was resonant as sirens, loudly said,

'We *know* the line, dear. What we don't know is
Which one of us has got to *say* the line.'

The Dog of Montargis had closed
    Before the week was up, despite
    The brilliant acting of the dogs.
    A dog had brought the villain down,
    A dog had saved the heroine,
    A dog had dragged out from a loft
    Her uncle's will and saved the day –
    And yet the public stayed away.
    The Manager now had to find
    Another play, and find it fast,
    To fill the bill. The Dog Man said
    'Well, why not give them *Hamlet*? I
    Have got some passing, tolerable
    Idea of how the story goes
    And I could get all Hamlet's lines
    There in the wings before each scene.
    Rely on me. I'd like the part,
    But more importantly, the dogs
    Could easily be trained, I'm sure.
    It's not so very different from
    The Dog of Montargis. Why not
    Let Hamlet have a faithful dog
    Who sniffs out old Polonius
    And whines whenever Claudius
    Looks at the Queen, and wags its tail
    Each time it sees Ophelia?
    And isn't there a graveyard scene?
    A dog could find a buried skull
    And put it down at Hamlet's feet.

And dogs could join the final brawl.'
But by late afternoon the play
Was looking less and less the thing.
The Dog Man said, 'It's looking bad.
We'll have to think of something else.
I've got the dogs trained, and I think
That they'd be all right on the night.
But Hamlet's part! Now there's the rub.
I've just now had a look at it
And I don't see how anyone
Could get those lines. I mean to say
He doesn't half go on, does he?
His bark's a lot worse than his bite.'

The power of art brought to the marketplace:
    When Mrs Siddons, shopping for a length
    Of calico, fiercely examined it
    With hands which nightly wrung with Duncan's blood,
    She asked with such dark force, '*But will it wash?*'
    The draper's boy fell fainting at her gaze.

To step out of a character,
    So often done as humour on the stage,
    May sometimes be that simple courtesy
    Required to explain an unavoidable
    Departure from the text. For instance, once
    The 'engagingly illiterate' John Rich,
    Bold Covent Garden manager
    And would-be actor, stepped offstage
    To knock the prompter to the floor
    And then returned to tell the audience
    'He interrupted me in my Grand Pause.'

'The Shrewsbury folk were generously disposed
  And when I found the entire house was booked
  I needed no persuasion to provide
  The usually frugal supper scene
  (In *High Life Below Stairs*) with something more
  Than was our usual staple (namely bread
  And chicken, toast, and water tinged with tea).
  Instead I had arranged for something hot
  With copious libations: first, a soup,
  Then half a cod, a saddle of best lamb,
  And apple tart with cream. And when at last
  The curtains opened on that splendid spread
  The savoury odours from such delicate
  And tempting viands thrilled those Shrewsbury folk
  Who may have never seen such banqueting
  Upon a stage.
            Alas! It is a rule
  That all performances should terminate
  By eleven of the clock. And so it was
  That just as Lady Charlotte and His Grace,
  The Duke, and old Sir Harry with their friends
  Sat down to supper, so the fatal clock
  Announced the hour. Our worthy manager,
  Perhaps assuming the applause was meant
  As a reproach at what they held to be
  His parsimony, or feeling suddenly
  An ebullition of bad temper, cried,
  'Bring down the curtain!' and required the band
  To play 'God Save the Queen'. The audience howled
  And we complained. But he put out the lights
  As resolute in this as was the Moor.
  In vain I asked that we might end the scene

And with it our repast on stage. But this
Earned nothing but a cutting negative.
And so, we gathered up our food and drink
And bore it to our hotel chamber, there
To finish it 'in measureless content'.

O'Rourke however told me that this coup
By management was nothing to a time
In Worcester. The occasion was his benefit.
The afterpiece was *Eugene Aram* – but
The actor playing Aram on the night
Was one who had a special weakness for
Long death scenes and could be relied upon
Never to shuffle off this mortal coil
In less than fifteen minutes. Thus on this night
He had his quietus – poison in a phial –
And leisurely began his long-drawn business.
Just then the clock struck eleven, and at once
The manager – bold Bennett – in a cloak
Came on and said, 'Ah! My good fellow, don't
Be troubled with that poison. I've good news.
You've been reprieved. And Madeleine the Fair
Is waiting to be married. Orchestra!
Strike up *All Troubles o'er, joys in Store*.
Ring down the curtain.' Down the curtain came
Much to old Aram's loudly voiced disgust
And cries of laughter from the audience.'

A curious casement opening on
    The old dichotomy between
    Appearance and reality,
    Or make-believe and truth, appeared
    When in the summer months the stage

Was opened upstage on the street –
Doors open, backdrops rolled aside –
And passing horse and carriage set the scene.
So audiences were beguiled,
Even distracted, by the flow
Of vehicles which might come and go.
But one mild evening even this
Perplexing casement was to be
Thrown even wider. In the play,
The Seven Brigands, five of them
Had ambushed young Antonio
Who bravely, single-handedly,
Engaged them with his sword. Just then
A dray was passing in the street.
The carter saw this cruel scene
And while his draught horse cropped the verge
(Where weeds were real and plentiful)
He gave a sudden lusty cry,
'Five against one is hardly fair!'
And leaping from his loaded dray,
Wielding a pole, joined in the fray.

For thirty-seven days and twenty hours
    The charming cantatrice from Drury Lane
    Was fearful she might not have brought enough
    Necessities of life for South Australia.
    On disembarking she was much surprised
    That here were streets and fine amenities
    Almost old London's equal. And the grapes!
    Her dressing room was garnished with a bunch
    So large it must have weighed some fifteen pounds.
    They showed her magpies. How the creatures sang,
    And one she watched perform stood on a cat(!)

Which seemed to sleep through its rendition of
'Pop Goes the Weasel', Australia's national song.
Her own performance at the Theatre Royal
In which she sang, to general acclaim,
'The Harp That Once', 'The Elixir of Love',
'O Steer My Bark to Erin's Isle', and then
Gave scenes from *Carmen* and *The Bohemian Girl* –
Was slightly marred by that pernicious trade,
Namely, of vendors selling ginger beer
Amongst the audience. Her cadence trill
Was three times interrupted on the night
By those explosive forces. Nonetheless,
Encores were called for and she sang an air
From *Hearts are Trumps* to very loud applause.
The only blemish, noted in the press,
Was caused by that Antipodean pest,
The mosquito, which delighted in her hair
And which she frequently must brush aside.
Her farewell night was like a string of pearls
With each pearl threatening to become a tear:
A nymph brought on a sheaf of flannel flowers,
And then the mayor gave her an emu's egg
Set on a silver stand. She made a speech
In which she said that never had she dreamt
That Adelaide would be so beautiful.

The author's dream (so rarely bearing fruit
    Not touched by fly or frost or hail or blight)
Of finding favour with the audience
Could scarcely take more gratifying form
Than at the opening of *Black Comedy*:
The author, seated in the audience,

    Observed in front of him a middle-aged,
    Stern gentleman fall sideways from his seat
    Into the aisle. He could not speak at first
    But pointed weakly at the stage. At last
    He managed to articulate these words:
    'Oh, stop! Please stop! I can't laugh any more.'

Some weeks before his final curtain fell
    Kean struggled to revive *Othello*. Hell
    And Heaven side by side stared from the pit,
    And in the shadowy wings the prompter sat
    With papers edged in black. Charles, his son,
    As Iago urged him on. And still Act One
    Took lifetimes to endure. He strove to reach
    The peaks of Act Two, then the farewell speech,
    With something of the old phosphoric fire.
    But at *Be sure thou prove my love a whore*,
    Which once had seized Creation in its jaws,
    He faltered. Then he fell. A flooding pause
    Enveloped him. He surfaced, but had thrown
    His arms around the shoulders of his son.
    He stared as one who reads the open sea,
    Then said, 'I am dying. Speak to them for me.'
    At last Iago carried him away
    And when a mortal came to end the play
    The audience, used to signs and wonders, left.

To swell the precious granaries of applause
    And guarantee the harvest every time,
    Dame Marie Tempest had decided on
    A simple ruse. Each time she went offstage
    She'd start the clapping from the wings herself,
    Assured the stalls would bear it like a torch

Up to the gallery. And furthermore
At curtain calls she had her maid send on
Her Sealyham dog, as if it followed her.
She'd turn and be surprised and shrug and smile
And take it in her arms. The audience
Would roar approval and this generally
Would lead to several further curtain calls.

The history of the struggle to invent
    A true vernacular Australian art
    Of humour could be said to reach a small
    Apotheosis in the following:
    To match Miss Hilda Talma's bicycle
    Which seems to ride in air without support,
    The famed Sheep Shearing Barber Shop Quartet,
    And Captain Winston's Laugh a Minute Seals,
    Fred Bluett at the Tivoli performs
    His famous *Salome* burlesque. He stands,
    His singlet lurid in a violet beam;
    With hairy arm he lifts the platter lid,
    Then brings the house down as he gives a cry
    And clasps a sheep's head to him as he dies.

In 1833 the Theatre Royal
    In George Street, Sydney, opened to acclaim.
    Henceforth the art of Theatre Criticism
    Would flourish hand in hand now with the Play,
    Its handmaiden, sometimes overleaping it.
    So after several years, the *Monitor*
    With much finesse reported on a farce,
    'Here Mrs Mackie acted what she could
    Remember of her part, and Mrs Dawes
    Spoke almost loud enough to be well heard.'

When Mrs Sarah Baker, Theatre Manager
　　At Rochester, devised her notices she cut
　　And pasted names and titles from old programme sheets;
　　This was because while she could read but passably
　　She never had acquired the art of penmanship.
　　She lived both for and in the theatre, sleeping there
　　And rising early to begin box office work
　　And raise the curtain on the theatre's crowded day.
　　Her true vocation was in taking the receipts
　　And greeting patrons at the door. Occasionally
　　She beat the drum or tolled the bell behind the scenes
　　When such embellishments were called for by the text,
　　And sometimes, ill-advisedly perhaps, she took
　　The role of prompter. One night when she held the book
　　For *Who's the Dupe?*, her actor, Gardiner,
　　(Who, seeking to impress, must speak some words of Greek)
　　Unfortunately had other matters on his mind
　　And, memory failing him, he glanced into the wings.
　　But Mrs Baker with a frowning, puzzled air
　　Stared at the page. When Gardiner whispered, 'What is the word?'
　　She whispered loudly back, 'It is a hard word.'
　　'Well,' Gardiner said, 'what is the next word after that?'
　　'It's harder.' Now the play had foundered on this pause.
　　'The next, then!' he cried loudly. Mrs Baker cried,
　　'It's harder still.' The audience by now
　　Were revelling in this.
　　　　　　　　　Perplexed beyond endurance then,
　　She flung the prompt book at him shouting, 'There now! There
　　Are all the words you're asking for. You take your choice.'
　　It has been said that Mrs Baker was the source
　　Of Dickens' Mrs Jarley in her Waxwork van.

From the Diary of One Upstaged:
> Tonight he spoiled my exit yet again.
> Tonight he coughed and killed my best laugh line.
> Tonight he quite deliberately destroyed
> My finest scene. Has he no sense of shame?
> But, ah! All this may change. In our new play,
> I see I have a quite substantial speech
> Downstage. The audience must be mine alone
> For he is upstage seated at a desk,
> His back turned, while he writes a letter. Ah!
> He is a fiend. *Tonight he drank the ink.*

The Restoration actor William Peer
> Achieved the rare distinction that his fame
> (Which was considerable) was seen to rest
> Entirely on the speaking of five lines.
> In three of these he took the character
> Of Prologue in the Play Within the Play
> In *Hamlet*. Here he spoke with such an air
> As managed to suggest that he alone
> Was merely imitating actors, while
> The company assembled was thus made
> To seem, by that modesty, more great and real.
> Here was a subtlety which, it was thought,
> Peer made his own, and this despite the fact
> That those three lines which made the Prologue's part,
>> *For us and for our tragedy,*
>> *Here stooping to your clemency*
>> *We beg your hearing patiently.*
> State nothing more than formal courtesies.
> The other portion of his repertoire
> In which he showed an equal excellence
> Were those two lines which Otway allocates

The Apothecary, in his *Caius Marius*.
Here he conveyed, in a most lamentable tone,
Reluctance to yield up the fatal draught,
Which circumstance must contradict:
> *My poverty but not my will consents.*
> *Take this, and drink it off; the work is done.*

So curiously disproportionate
Were these short roles to their enduring fame,
That Management, regarding this as proof
Of his Propriety, conferred on him
The further offices of Property Man.
Thus he became responsible for all
Such tools and implements the play demands,
As billet-doux, false money, poison, wine,
Pomatum, scrolls of parchment, truncheons, sticks,
Tin thunderbolts, daggers and wooden legs,
And other sundries for the Prompter's call.
This elevation had a strange effect.
For just as it may happen that a man
May lose some virtue in prosperity
So this good fortune led to Peer's demise:
His increased comforts made him corpulent
And so too merry for the Prologue's part;
Nor could he now seem cogent with the force
Of wan distress to play the Apothecary.
In short, we see in Peer the curious case
Of fame in one adjudged to speak five lines
More beautifully than any other man,
Yet whose success leads to its own decline.
Five lines sustained him till his seventieth year
At which time this calamity, it seems,
Contributed to the shortening of his days.

When Mrs Siddons left
> The splendours of her lasting presence on the stage
> She still gave salon readings. Haydon was at one:
>> – She acts all of *Macbeth*
> Far better than poor Kean or Kemble ever did,
> The awe this woman still inspires is palpable.
>> She read today then paused,
> At which the men retired to tea. And while we were
> All eating toast and tinkling cups on saucers, she
>> Began again. It was
> As if the bell rang out for mass in Spain. Noise ceased.
> We slunk back to our seats, some with the very toast
>> Still brittle in their mouths,
> Afraid to bite. How curious it was to see
> Sir Thomas Lawrence, in this same predicament
>> Bite by degrees then stop
> For fear of making too much crackle, while his eyes
> Now filled with water from this difficult constraint.
>> And still to hear her voice
> Her 'eye of newt and toe of frog' as through his tears
> The straining Lawrence takes a furtive bite, looks awed,
>> And holds his listening pose.
> I felt that I was witnessing an oddity,
> A curious allegory of the senses, a dispute
>> Between the arts of Sight and Sound.

Sometimes a simple phrase floats from the page
> And carries with it like an atmosphere
> Or ceiling Cupids trailing garland flowers
> An echo of the voice which spoke the words.
> Thus Edith Evans recollecting Shaw,
> 'He flirted with me. And he kissed me once.
> *But I derived no benefit from it.*'

Young Henry Siddons, witness to
His mother's genius, and
The ambiguous fault line pressed between
Truth and illusion on the stage:
'When Mrs Siddons' son, aged eight,
Was acting in the play with her,
Despite rehearsals, on the night
Her death scene drew from him real tears
Which nothing could abate until
The curtain fell. She rose, she moved;
She took his hand to comfort him.
Her art has been described as truth
And daylight mingled on the stage
(In Kitty Clive's admiring words).
On this occasion truth shone out
But dappled in the daylight's glare.'

An impoverished actor:
'Having a family to support
I used to walk to Croydon every day
Ten miles and back, rehearsing on
One penny's worth of oats and one of milk;
This must sustain me until opening night
When gentlemen in the gallery pelted us
With mutton pies. At first we were
Upset, but soon enjoyed these critical crumbs
In comfort underneath the stage.'

Peg Woffington had *mastered* – so to speak –
The breeches part, *Sir Harry Wildair*, rake,
So winningly, with such persuasive charm
That one night in the Green Room she exclaimed,
'Well surely, by my conscience, I believe

That half the men tonight have taken me
As one of their own sex.' To which James Quin
Admiringly but tartly said he thought
The other half could claim the contrary.

'George Frederick Cooke, much idolised by Kean
    For his ferocity, could never quite
    Be sure if his expression were precise
    As he believed it should be. Once, to test
    The catalogue of passions of the heart
    Fuming like vapour from his countenance,
    He fixed one young admirer with his gaze;
    He formed his features, then triumphantly
    Demanded of his audience, 'Now Sir,
    What passion do you see?' The young man said,
    'That is revenge, Sir, frighteningly expressed,'
    At which Cooke shouted, 'Sir, you lie! That's love!
    You err in reading from this folio.'
    In similarly optimistic vein,
    The instruction to an actor in his troupe
    By Harley Granville Barker: 'At this point
    I want you, when you enter, to convey
    A man who's deeply steeped in Tennyson.'
    Or J.M. Barrie who on hearing this
    Said to another member of the cast,
    'I want you, when you enter, to convey
    A man whose brother lives in Surbiton.'

At Garrick's funeral the air was close
    With memories of noble deeds and deaths,
    Gestures and speeches, presences. The bell
    Tolled like a long soliloquy. Dense crowds
    Fell back before the entering black cortège.

I undertook for Garrick to enquire
Of Johnson (as of the Delphic Oracle)
His true opinions of his (Garrick's) fame.
I took an early opportunity
Of waiting on him and was pleased to find
Him in a good and social humour. Then
I soon began a conversation which
Led naturally to Garrick and the stage.
I made remarks about his excellence
Amongst our actors and I said
'But pray now, Dr Johnson do you think
That he deserves his high celebrity?'
'Oh, sir,' said he, 'he certainly deserves
All that he has acquired, for having seized
The very soul of Shakespeare, and
For having thus embodied it in himself,
And for expanding its chief glories through the world.'

The bells massed like clouds which hide the sun.
Burke was seen in tears. And Sheridan
Stood wide-eyed in the candles' catafalque.

His Shakespeare Jubilee was notable
For speeches, odes, effusions, notables,
Processions, banquets, fetes, triumphal cars,
A recitation, masquerade and ball,
But not a single line of Shakespeare's Works.
Now as if to exact some recompense, the rain
Began. The ostrich plumes, brocades,
The shepherdesses' silks and satin shoes,
The catherine-wheels, flambeaux and laurel wreaths
Were drenched in quite unprecedented rain.
The Avon, that 'with gentle murmur glides',

Soon burst its banks engulfing carriages…
Then on the third day, by mid-afternoon,
The rain retreated into heavy skies.
The colt race could be run, and nightfall brought
Its sky with sifted yeast of fireworks.
At the Rotunda (now accessible)
The masquerade went on till dawn
And Mrs Garrick 'danced a minuet
Beyond description gracefully'.

Devised by Sheridan, the funeral order read:
'Four men in mourning with their staffs enswathed
In black, on horseback. Six more ditto
Bearing mourning cloaks et cetera.
A man to bear the pennon and the scarf.
Two walking as supporters. Six in cloaks
Solemn as before. Surcoat of arms.
Helmet with crest. The wreath and mantlet. All
Surmounted by black ostrich feathers. Dark
Escutcheons. The hearse bearing the corse.'

O think, Peg, of the many nights we passed
Together in delicious happiness.
I often wish my tongue had blistered first
Before I spoke the words which made you say
Thy smock should never more be pressed to mine,
For then you left me, never to return…

When three or four are on the stage with him
He is attentive to the others' speech
Nor drops his character when he has done
By either looking with severe contempt
On an inferior performance

Or unnecessary spitting, sighing
Or the invention of distracting business.

Clouds hid the sun. The bells were silenced.
The bishop's solemn tone
Was audible in every particle.

Johnson, The epitaph:
'I am disappointed by that stroke of death
Which has eclipsed the gaiety of nations
And impoverished the public stock of harmless pleasure.'

Hannah More to her sister:
    … We hurried in a hackney coach
Dreading to be too late. The bells
Above St Martin's and the Abbey rang,
Increasing our alarm. And when we reached
The cloisters we found multitudes
All seeking entry. We of course
Had tickets from the Bishop but, alas,
We gave these to a man who let us in
But showed us to a sombre tower
Then locked the door. A dark staircase
Consisting of a hundred stone steps
Led nowhere and we ran back down again
And hammered on the door. The bells
Rang still, so many that there seemed
No space between the sounds. In agony
We cried and beat upon the door. At last
A guardian angel – so it seemed –
Unlocked the door. We begged him to help us
Find somewhere in the Abbey where we might
See something of the grave. He asked

To see our Bishop's ticket – Ah!
We said that we had given it away
To someone in the crowd, we knew not whom.
He had no reason to believe
And yet he saw truth in our grief
And took us safely through the swelling crowd
And put us in a little gallery above
The grave, where we could see and hear
As clearly as if we had been
In someone's parlour rather than the Abbey.
Sometimes small things affect us powerfully;
I found myself gazing upon
The Handel monument, the stone
Scroll floating from his hand: *I know that my*
Redeemer liveth. Suddenly, at three,
The great doors opened with a noise
That shook the roof. The organ led
The choir in Handel's anthem, solemn strains
Like an Archangel's trump. The choir advanced
In hoods and capes; then Sheridan
As the chief mourner; then (alas!)
The body – whose it seemed impossible
To credit with belief. Ten noblemen,
Pall bearers, gentlemen, the rest
All friends and mourners – nowhere there
A dry eye; even players, bred to the art
Of counterfeiting, shed their genuine tears.
The service passed. The Bishop read
In low and solemn voice, to laud
The voice which was the essence of our age.
Each syllable hung like a water drop,
And how I felt it as it fell!

Thus did the world pass from the world.
And yet that very night those self-same crowds
Were at the playhouse revelling. That night
The Pantheon was filled, as if
Nothing passed ever from the world.
And afterwards the Bishop's lady came
Inviting us into the Deanery.
With others of the actor's friends
We were brought to her dressing room
But seeing us incapable of speech
She very kindly sent up wine and cake
And would not interrupt our grief.
I caught no cold and got home safe.
On Wednesday to Mrs Garrick's house.
She bore her grief with great tranquillity
But what was my surprise at length
To see her go into the room
And bed in which he died that fortnight. She
Took sad delight in it beyond
Expression. And the following day
I asked her how she could go through with it?
She told me 'Very well', that first she had prayed
With great composure, then she kissed the bed
And lay down with a sad and sweet repose.

The evening being sultry, and the stage
   Oppressive, Mrs Siddons felt a thirst
So overwhelming that her dresser sent
A boy in haste to fetch a pint of beer.
Meanwhile *Macbeth* continued. When the boy
Returned with frothing pitcher to the wings
He found no one he recognised and asked,

'Where is this Mrs Siddons who wants beer?'
A stage-hand pointed to the stage where now
The murderess was walking in her sleep.
The boy walked up to her, without the least
Awareness of this impropriety,
And stood there with the pitcher losing froth
And said, 'Are you the Mrs Siddons who
Sent out for beer?' She waved the boy away
Still in her grandest manner several times
Without effect. At last behind the scenes,
By dint of gestures, beckoning and cries,
The cast succeeded in retrieving him,
But not before the audience dissolved
In laughter which the actress could not quell
For several minutes' dark solemnities.

Will Shakespear having fled from Warwickshire
    To escape the charge of stealing landed deer
    His first expedient was to wait outside
    The play-house door and hold their horses for
    Those patrons who had ridden to the play,
    And who did not have servants of their own.
    He soon was so conspicuous for his care
    That every man alighting called for him
    Wanting no other. When Will Shakespear had
    More horses in his hand than he could hold
    He hired boys to wait upon these herds,
    Which boys soon earned the name of *Shakespear's Boys*.
    In time Will Shakespear moved to higher things
    (Inside the theatre) but those boys
    Retained the appellation. (Johnson adds these facts
    To those told in the *Life* by Nicholas Rowe.)

One might adduce some further lesson here
Whereby *to hold one's horses* might be seen
To signify creation's first restraint
Essential to all subsequent flood-bursts
And licensing each future masterpiece.

'In 1822 the venerable
    And much respected Mrs Garrick died,
While seated in her armchair in the room
Where she received her guests. Queen Charlotte had
Been one of those, and finding her engaged
In peeling onions for a pickle, asked
To be allowed a knife to peel them too.
Just after Mrs Garrick's death, I went
To the Adelphi. There George Harris (one
Of several confidential servants) said,
"The funeral day is not yet fixed. But would
You like to see her? She is in her coffin."
I said, "Yes, I would." On entering
The back room on the first floor where she died
I found two female servants at her side.
I made a drawing and enquired of them,
"Pray, tell me, why is the coffin draped with sheets?"
"They are their wedding sheets (now winding sheets)
In which both had expressed their wish to die."
Some forty-three years earlier – a life! –
The actor died. And on his memory
She lived as tranquilly as she now died,
Borne always on the breath of his voiced lives.'

A certain Dr Kennedy,
    Friend both to Garrick and to Sterne,
    Was nonetheless a charlatan,

To this extent that he devised
A method of attracting fame:
He had secured a front row seat;
Each evening at the theatre he
Would regularly be called away,
Just as the play began, by one
Who by arrangement loudly cried,
'Is Dr Kennedy in the house?
We must find Dr Kennedy,
Who is wanted urgently.' Then he
Would rise and thus conspicuous
Would leave in haste. This had the effect
Of eliciting from the audience
Of lords and ladies the response,
'Bless me! That Dr Kennedy
Has half the patients in the town.'
At length however this device
Grew less efficient. Every night
'We're seeking Dr Kennedy.
Oh, where is Dr Kennedy?'
Rang fifty times through all the house,
From humorists in the Gallery.

The invention of fresh business,
    The offspring of necessity,
    Is nicely instanced in the play
    The Constant Husband. On the ground,
    A letter which to impel the plot
    Must be picked up. Both actresses
    Now stout (who long before in youth
    Had outshone Garrick's *Benedict*)
    Discovered neither dared bend down

To pick it up. The scene was saved
When Mrs Pritchard improvised
(As haughty mistress to her maid),
'Well, Madame Pert, since you refuse
To pick this letter up, I'll find
Someone who will,' and rang the bell.
The prompter was alert, and sent
Another servant on. And soon
The letter having lodged its barb,
The comedy went on its way.

Of famous dog performances,
The Dog of Montargis drew crowds;
But rivalling that the pair of dogs
Who graced *The Hindoo Robber* as
The Spotted Leopards of the Plains:
To end Act Two, one of this pair
Is shot by hunters, and expires
(After much staggering) on a rock
And in its twitching tail displays
Such virtuosic nonchalance
As to elicit wild applause.
Eventually (said Alfred Bunn,
Who should be some authority
On dogs, since he it was who bit
Macready's finger in a fight
About abridgements to a play),
The second leopard, hearing this
Night after night, and filled perhaps
With jealousy, careered onstage
And outdid all that went before
By dying most extravagantly.

The audience was doubly pleased,
Particularly as in its throes
The spotted leopard cambric split
And its own tail broke through and wagged
Beside its spotted replica.
This latter dog (a Newfoundland
Named Carlos) then went on to star
Out-acting the entire cast
And saved a mediocre piece,
The Caravan, which Sheridan
Had hitched to the fate of Drury Lane.
While Carlos took more curtain calls
To cries of *Good dog*, Sheridan
Called 'My preserver!' from the wings.
The author rose to take a bow
But Sheridan (solvent at last)
Said 'No! Not you. I mean the dog.'

On the emollient of vanity:
While Mr Seyton who should have appeared
Was laughing in the Green Room still, Charles Kean
Strode up and down the stage in furious rage,
'Where is he? Send him on. I'll savage him.'
After a long delay Seyton arrived
And said, 'What is your Grace's will?' gasping
In trepidation. Kean glared vengefully.
'Saw you the weird sisters?' – a simple prompt
To which the other should say, 'No, my Lord.'
But with an impulse to make recompense
Young Seyton blurted out, 'Oh, yes my Lord.'
Taken aback Kean swore, 'The devil you did.
If so, where are they then?' Now quite unmanned,

Poor Seyton said, 'I'll show your Majesty
If you'll just deign to step around the corner.'
The scene limped to a close. Offstage Charles Kean
Attacked. But Seyton was surprisingly
Resourceful. 'Sir, I know the blame is mine.
And yet the fault, sir – with respect – was yours.'
'Mine, sir?' 'Yes. I was standing in the wings,
Watching the scene, and you so magnetised,
So dazzled me with those effulgent rays
Which emanated from your piercing eyes,
That I was quite unable to perform…'
Kean melted and betrayed a fleeting smile.
'Well then, dear boy, don't let it happen again.'

With Charles and Nelly Kean was seen again
    The business Mrs Siddons had devised
    For double bills. The first (a tragedy)
    Ends with the death of Charles Kean's character.
    He lies in state and, weeping, Mrs Kean
    Is being led off-stage; she suddenly turns,
    Breaks free and runs back to her husband. 'Oh!'
    She cries, 'Oh Charley! Say you are not dead.'
    'But deuce a bit! You're squashing me, my dear.'
    'Oh never mind that, Charley. Tell me once again
    You are not dead.' 'But Nelly, can't you see?
    I'm telling you. There, there now. Don't you fret
    But run away and dress as Violante
    For our next play.' 'Good Gracious!' Nelly cries,
    Recovering and springing up. 'How strange –
    I'd quite forgotten that! The second play!
    Ladies and gentlemen, I take my leave
    But soon we will return with Comedy!'

And with a bow she makes her cheery way
Towards the dressing room and Interval.

More instances of stepping in and out
    Of rôles (a notable phenomenon
    Which makes the stage a kind of overcoat):
    First… In the provinces a memory loss,
    The prompter absent at the inn next door,
    The play so popular that the audience
    Supplies the line in charming dialect.
    The actor steps downstage and doffs his cap
    And says, 'I thank you all, my messmates. Memory
    Cannot bear endless repetition. Well!
    Let us resume,' and once more wears the coat.
    Or, more dramatically, the Quarrel Scene
    In *Julius Caesar* was auspiciously
    Proceeding, when a bagman drunkenly
    Insulted Brutus and disturbed the peace.
    That Brutus now stepped easily from the rôle
    And said, 'Excuse me, brother Cassio,'
    And leapt into the boxes, seized the man
    And propelled him by his neck-scruff to the doors
    And thence into the street. Wiping his hands
    He came back to the stage to assume the cloak
    Once more, as if nothing had intervened.
    Another instance, rather more extreme:
    The same heroic actor (Paumier,
    This time a strapping Hamlet six feet tall)
    Was interrupted in his final duel
    By rowdy students jeering from their box.
    For now he waited patiently until
    The afterpiece in which he cracks a whip

              (Petruchio at the sumptuous wedding feast
              In *Katherine and Petruchio)*. In this
              Again he heard the derision of that crowd.
              At once he strode out to the box and seized
              The chief offender, dragged him to the stage
              And whipped him roundly, throwing him at last
              Into the orchestra. Blandly he spoke:
              'You may have taken some exception to
              My Hamlet's foil play, but at least I think
              I've shown some expertise here with the whip.
              And so I trust we may resume the stage,
              Act in our roles and happily end the piece.'

The first performance of *Macbeth* in France
              Was flawed. The English company had to use
              Old scenery from Italian operas;
              The *mise en scène* lacked heath and lightning bolt
              And castle, while the witches had to dance
              Without the aid of music. Yet at times
              The language had the power to astound –
              The ingredients for the witch's cauldron brought
              A cry of '*Oh, Mon Dieu! Quel drôle mélange!*'
              A tendency towards the statuesque
              Shown by Macready led Stendhal to say
              'He holds himself as if the pit were filled
              With painters.' Others too remarked
              The excessive prolongation of the pose.
              Edward Fitzgerald had already said
              'He would stand with his mouth wide open, till
              I longed to pitch things into it from the Pit.'
              Despite dissenting voices, many thought
              The strangling in *Othello* in poor taste,

And Delacroix urged the Academy
To halt 'such foreign importations') still
Shakespearian fever gripped the capital.
And Harriet Smithson as its brightest star,
Who was for Berlioz a lightning-bolt,
Indulged a quite Shakespearian excess
By painting on her carriage the device,
In scrolls of gilt, 'My kingdom for a horse.'

The curious power of unexpected facts
    Which sail across the stage on soaring-wires
    Flies from the page.
                   These instances float out:
That Margaret Rutherford flew on such wires
In *Alice in Wonderland*, doubling the rôle
With Sybil Thorndike; that on her grave
Was carved the single legend, *Blithe Spirit*;
That Stringer Davis died the following year,
Was buried in pyjamas, with, in the pocket,
A mysterious letter from John Gielgud.
She said,
             'To fly on wires from the wings
Across the stage and disappear again
Was wonderful, like nothing else I've known.'
She said, 'I always found a cape would help
The character; in fact I must have worn
More capes than anyone but Dracula.'
Such facts may lie long hidden, lost in books,
Until their pages open in the breeze
Which brings a sudden yacht upon their waves.

When Mrs Siddons travelled north
    To act in *Douglas* (by a Scottish bard)
    Great national pride was simmering
    And someone shouted from the Pit,
    'Whaur's yer Wully Shakespeare noo?'

Dame Edith Evans used to say
    If when the play is over you don't walk
    For several blocks still quite unsure
    In which direction you are meant to go
    Then your performance was not good enough.
    A similar distraction may be seen
    In Mrs Siddons after her *Macbeth*:
    Returning to her dressing-room she stood
    Before her mirror. That bright night remained.
    Again she said aloud in just the voice
    She'd used: *Here's the smell of blood still*,
    And stared into the glass. So she stood.
    Her dresser said, 'Dear me, ma'am, this is strange
    And violent, for I vow it was not blood
    But rose-pink mixed with water – for I saw
    The property man mix it before my eyes.'

A tendency which Hannah More deplored
    In current fashion was the fondness for
    A veritable salad worn on heads,
    Where vine and cress and fruit and vegetable
    Were raised to ludicrous excess. She wrote
    Of some eleven ladies at one place
    Who had amongst them teetering on their heads
    'An acre and a half of shrubbery
    With grass plots, tulip beds and peonies
    And kitchen gardens.'

                It is said
  That, wishing to cut down 'with trenchant scythe
  A harvest of follies and absurdities',
  She encouraged Garrick to appear on stage
  With an entire vegetable crop as hat
  Complete with 'glass cucumber frames set off
  With pendant carrots at each ear'.

Along the labyrinthine way
  Of Sight and Sound, one avenue
  May sometimes lead to puzzlement
  Finding a place where nothing seems
  Familiar, where sense of place
  Seems strangely overturned. The light
  May seem excessive, or a sound
  Persist without apparent source –
  The kind of place vivid yet strange
  Which Wells found once and never found
  Again beyond the wall. Of course
  Such dislocation frequently
  May happen in the theatre. There
  The light, a sudden hush, a pause,
  A chance inflexion of the voice
  May easily induce it. So
  (This is the very archetype
  Of such experience) Hannah More
  Deciding on a whim to go
  To hear the mad-scene in her play
  (*Percy*, a tragedy) arrived
  And, entering a box, was plunged
  At once into a startlement:
  'I'd come for Mrs Barry, who

Is very fine and though the piece
Is my own nonsense, nonetheless
I always see that part with pleasure.
I looked down on the stage and saw
The scene was in a prison, and
The heroine had on a gown
Of linen! I was stunned and thought
I'd lost my senses. Then a man
In regimentals came downstage
And looking up began to sing
How happy could I be with either…
I stared and rubbed my eyes, convinced
That I was in a dream. (Why did
It take me such a time to see?)
For soon I realised the play
Had been *The Beggar's Opera* – because
The principal was taken ill
And hand-bills were distributed,
I found, to announce another play.
I came away still dazed, that scene
Imprinted with such clarity,
As if I'd crossed a stream – and on
The further shore nothing was the same.'

Peg Woffington had come
    To gain an audience
    With John Rich (theatre manager):
    Rich was reclining on a Couch,
    His left Leg lolling on the right,
    A Playbook in one hand
    And in the other a China Cup
    From which he sipped some Tea.

About him, *round* him, *on* him were
Seven-and-twenty Cats
Of every Colour, Size and Age.
Several stared him in the Face,
Some ate the Buttered Toast
Out of his Mouth, some licked
The Cream out of a Cup,
Some frisked about, some lay,
Some perched upon his Knee
And some upon his Head.
The Manager was much impressed:
'It was most fortunate indeed
That I was not susceptible;
Had it been otherwise
I should have found it difficult
To keep my equanimity
While still conducting business with
This charming Composite
Of Circe and Calypso with
The majesty of Juno, charm
Of Hebe, and the loveliness
Of Venus stepping from her shell.
Her signing in my Company
Was managed purringly.'

'Cat' Harris famous for his mimicking
    Of cats and, in particular, degrees
    And subtleties of mewing, was engaged
    By Samuel Foote to sing a cat duet
    (With Shuter) in his latest comedy.
    On seeking Harris in his rooms,
    Not knowing where he lived, Shuter began

A caterwauling solo in the street,
At which shrill signal Harris looking out
Replied in kind with complicated cries
As if a full moon and a catnip crop
Converged. Thus they met.
In Foote's advertisements a cautionary note
Was sounded: *Ladies and Gentlemen are warned
To leave their Lapdogs and their Spaniels
Safely at home because of Cats.*

The Duke of Rutland (aptly named),
The Manners family patriarch,
Was one of several who were fanned
And flamed by Peggy Woffington.
One night a voice called from the pit,
'Whom did you sleep with last night, Peg?'
And she in mid-line turned, and paused,
And smiled, and murmured, 'Manners, you dog!'

The Duke of Clarence, formerly
Regarded as a dedicated rake,
Became in Mrs Jordan's arms
An almost dedicated husband. Twenty years
Brought forth ten children and a galaxy
Of triumphs on the stage. Her voice
(Wrote Hazlitt) was *a cordial to the heart
Because it came from it, rich, full,
And like the luscious juice of the ripe grape,
To hear whose laugh was to drink nectar.*
But Mrs Jordan could be vocal too
In matters of the heart and state;
For when, allegedly, the King announced a plan
To halve her thousand pounds annuity

(Paid on his son's behalf), she tore
And sent part of a playbill back to him.
It read, *No moneys are refundable
Once the curtain has been raised.*

An Irish actor lay at death's stage-door
    And, almost past the power of speech, received
    A visit from a worthy clergyman.
    The good man strove to help him recognise
    The grave, momentous stage he ventured on;
    He raised his voice and said, 'Consider, Sir,
    You have a very serious part to play –'
    The actor rallied briefly in his bed:
    'I wish that you would *newly cast* the piece
    And give the role to someone else, for I
    Could never in my life play *serious parts*.'

Sir Richard Steele tells – in *The Tatler* –
    Of a poor actor having no new roles
    Who fell into a serious decline.

    As such he was thought worthy of the part
    Of the impoverished and starving apothecary
    In *Romeo and Juliet*. Success

    Restored him to himself and equally
    Disqualified him from that wretched role.
    And so, unfit to take that part, he fell

    Once more into his former grave decline.
    Then this impoverishment in turn again
    Made him ideal to play the apothecary.

Ellen Kean to Mary Kean:

'For four long hours we passed through countryside
About as interesting as Salisbury Plains
Without Stonehenge. On every side all seems
"Flat and unprofitable." But as we reach
This place 2,000 ft above the sea
The flats are less unprofitable, for here
Are excellent sheep walks and the scattered mines.
Within a mile or so of Ballarat
The same monotony prevails. Some hills
Appear and tangled tracts of forest gums,
With here and there an iron hut, and now
The Forest Home Hotel. The gum tree stems
Grow out in every way, lacking all form.
We're told a forest of these eucalypts
Is like a Cathedral aisle but I cannot
Find beauty in their twisting, tangling mass.
We saw almost as many magpies too;
They are less handsome than our magpies, both
In shape and plumage, and are black where ours
Are white and white where ours are black. Also
We saw rosellas. But the Forest Home
Is *excellent*. They gave us a good soup,
Stewed native sole and veal and river duck,
An excellent light pudding, apple tarts,
Good sherry and good soda water too.
The air is sharp and cold but so far seems
Invigorating. This whole town is now
But ten years old and yet already is
Much fallen off. The people here complain
Of bad times. Gold, at first, was everywhere,
All "surface gold", and they ran mad with luck

And in bravado would eat five pound notes
In bread and butter – money sandwiches –
But then all came to quartz and stone and grief.
And yet, with our arrival here, it seems
The theatre flourishes. Just yesterday
In Melbourne Mr Coppin gave a speech
And said that Charles Kean had enabled him
To pay to all his sundry creditors
Their twenty shillings in the pound. In fact
We find in Mr Coppin nothing less
Than honesty and cheerfulness despite
The reputation which preceded him.
The prices here are high: ten shillings, box;
Six shillings, stalls; three shillings, gallery.
We signed today for California.
God bless you darling. Papa is so well.'

'This matter too,' said someone in our box,
   'They order differently in France.
The French do not approve of deaths on stage,
A view voiced by the censuring cries
Which greeted Desdemona's strangling, long drawn-out,
When first it came to Paris. Thus
The French observe a custom which avoids
Such gross infringements. So, it seems,
That in the opera *Artaxerxes* when
The hero Artabanes falls,
Slain, into the arms of courtiers,
The actor gives a little kick
Just as the curtain falls, to indicate
That *he has not died on the stage.*
This artifice speaks of the differences
Between the French stage and our own.'

Charles Kean to Mary Kean:
'... I am so overoccupied
That I must write quite briefly. I shall be
Delighted to escape these Colonies. I neither like
The climate or the people. And the flies!
While spiders crawl upon one's pillow and mosquitoes swarm
In myriads, the flies are like a plague.
At breakfast I am forced to place my saucer on my cup
And make the hastiest snatches at my tea
To stop the flies from falling into it. The days are cool
But still these creatures do not go away.
I stood Godfather, and your mother Godmother, today
To a baby christened Charles Edward Kean –
His lungs are powerful enough. He squalled without a pause.
But soon we leave for California.
Tonight we have to play in acts from *four* of Shakespeare's plays
To celebrate his anniversary,
So there's a long hard night ahead for both of us.
I cannot wait to be at home and taking my farewell
Upon a stage far, far away from here.
Do you know of an insect, named a mantis, like a kind
Of grasshopper? Well, one of these just fell
On to my morning paper as I sat reading in bed,
The creature wrestling with a fly it held
In its long arms. Such are the pleasures of Australian life.'

'In all the annals of great travesties
  I offer *Romeo and Juliet*
  Played as a comedy with interludes
  Of dance and song, an ending without deaths
  And language "partly that of Shakespeare" – this
  Put up on alternating nights

With the original, at Drury Lane.'
The speaker settled back and lit a pipe
Assured that he had won the day – until
A second then proposed the following:
'In 1810 when Mr Elliston
Acquired the Surrey Theatre he announced
*Macbeth As Altered From the Shakespeare Text
By Mr Lawler, Introducing Rhyme,*
The qualities of which one distich tells –
*Is this a dagger which I see before me?
My brains are scattered in a whirlwind stormy.*'

Accounts of Mrs Jordan's *voice*
   Are as many as they are perplexed
   To express the inexpressible.
   Silver is the epithet
   Most commonly recurring. Yet
   Specific attributes dissolve
   Into the general: *Sweetness, Light,
   Delicious echoes, Melody*,
   A *Brimming* as of cups poured full.
   The Old Playgoer treasured her:
   'I know the simile is stale
   But I can think of nothing more
   Approaching Mrs Jordan's voice
   Than that beguiling *jug jug jug*
   Of nightingales when May unclouds
   Her brightest moon and all her flowers
   Are sweetest… I cannot forget
   An enigmatic catch, a slight
   Provincialism in her words,
   A breadth which, just perceptible,

Sprang with her celebrated laugh;
Thus such a word as *both*, which she
Would almost render *boath*, then seems
To sound the only way it should…
That voice was full and sweet, yet *stole*,
And, never *penetrating, flowed*
About us like some vaporous rain;
Or else, as Shakespeare illustrates
One sense by dwelling on another,
"It came o'er the ear like the sweet south
That hath breathed upon a bank of violets".
And still she was, as Rosalind
Was by Orlando said to be,
"The inexpressive she." (And yet
What memories we harbour still
Of Mrs Jordan's Rosalind;
There never was, and never shall,
Nor ever could be such a Rosalind!)'
And so, *to illustrate one sense*
By dwelling on another, here
Perhaps we still may catch the sound
Of Mrs Jordan's laughing voice
As if by synaesthesia
As in this story from her times:
'An Irish baronet one day remarked
He had acquired a powerful telescope.
"You see yon church," he said, "a half mile off?
It shimmers, just discernible, and yet
When I observe it through my telescope
It floats so near I hear the organ play."'

When Kynaston played women's roles, King Charles
> Was much amused (the play being delayed)
> To hear the manager apologise:
> *The Queen was not yet shaved.*
> And Kynaston, whom Pepys professed to find
> *The loveliest of women he had seen*
> Was sought by ladies to accompany them
> In their carriages after the play.
> But Pepys was also captive to Nell Gwynn.
> *When visiting the tiring room*
> *Where Nell was dressing and was all unready*
> *And is very pretty, prettier than I thought.*

Boswell: *Garrick is not himself tonight.*
> Johnson: *No.* But Garrick suddenly
> Began to act superbly. Boswell: *Why!*
> *Did you observe how greatly he has changed*
> *And for the better?* Johnson: *Sir, did you*
> *Observe that he took on a higher style*
> *When Edmund Burke arrived and took his seat?*

When Mrs Siddons came to call
> It happened that there was no chair
> Until another could be brought.
> And Dr Johnson was *gallant*
> And said, 'Madam, you who have
> So often caused the want of seats
> For others will the more readily
> Excuse the want of one yourself.'

The impulse to return, to live again
> One's former triumphs on the glittering stage,
> An impulse Hazlitt saw and so deplored

In Mrs Siddons, was in a sense surpassed
By Mrs Jordan, she whose silver voice
Laid down bright trails like travelling moonlit waves.
Soon after her obscure last days in France,
James Boaden, her biographer, was half-
Convinced that it was she who reappeared
In Piccadilly, one calm evening:
A lady suddenly stood by my side.
She wore a glass upon a chain of gold
And used this to assist her sight. By chance
We both gazed through the window of a shop
At shadowy prints and books. She did not speak
But dropped a long white veil across her face
As if not wishing to be recognised.
And yet the notion seized me forcibly
That it was she – once more upon this stage.
Her daughter too believed, 'to her entire
Conviction', that she saw her in the Strand
After the sad reports arrived from France.

A curious case of Nature *in extremis*
    If not *imitating*, then assisting Art:
    The final uses of George Frederick Cooke,
    Inebriate, tragic Tragedian,
    Revered and said by Edmund Kean to be
    'The greatest creature ever to walk the earth',
    A toe bone from whose last remains Kean had
    Extracted at the actor's exhumation – this
    Kept with him everywhere and shown with pride
    Until his wife at length threw it away
    Into a well.
                  But now, an element

Of irony must be allowed, which rests
Upon the judgement, generally agreed,
That Cooke's own *Hamlet* was amongst the worst
In memory, so forthright was he. Thus
There is an added strangeness in the case.
For from this exhumation, secretly,
Cooke's skull had been removed and thence
Had passed into a Doctor Francis' care,
His friend of many years. Nearby
A theatre benefit was announced, the play
Was *Hamlet*; on that night, discovering
The lack, a stage-hand ran to that doctor's rooms
To secure a skull to serve the graveyard scene.
And Doctor Francis later wrote, 'Alas!
Poor Yorick! I was then compelled to lend
The noble head of George Frederick Cooke,
The finest actor ever posthumously
To appear in that most enigmatic play!'

Excesses which all greatness must engender:
The *Irish Post*, 1790 –
'On Saturday, in the tearful character
Of Isabella, Mrs Siddons shone;
From panegyrics heard persistently
In London we were taught to expect
A heavenly angel. But we were surprised
Into an awful joy when we beheld
A mortal goddess. She was nature itself.
She was the most exquisite work of art.
She was the very daisy, tuberose,
Sweet-briar, primrose, gillyflower, rose,
Furze-blossom, rosemary, auricula,

    Wallflower; in short
    She was the bouquet of Parnassus, not
    Forgetting too the holy three-leafed shamrock.'

'Our great Macready was preparing *Lear*.
    Our property-man was charged to send a map
    Amongst the many articles required
    (For Lear to allocate his provinces).
    Our property man, being illiterate,
    Read "mop" for "map" and on the night
    When Lear in solemn state upon his throne
    Calls for a map, a noble entered, knelt
    And gave the ancient King a curling mop.
    Macready, startled, dragged that nobleman,
    His mop accompanying him, into the wings
    While actors and the audience alike
    Enjoyed that sudden sunshower of delight
    Quite unexpected in the whole of *Lear*.'

A note on Mrs Barry:
              On stage
    Her tenderness was said to be
    So natural that she wept real tears
    And even under rouge she could
    Be seen to turn as white as snow.

One night when Macklin with a friend
    Was seated in the audience
    A man stood up in front of him,
    His person being rather large,
    And quite cut off their line of sight.
    The actor felt the usual fire
    But mastered it this time. He tapped

The shoulder of the gentleman
And gently asked,
>*Should anything*
Of interest happen on the stage
To let them be apprised of it
Since at the present they must be
Dependent totally upon
His kindness in relaying it.

Sheridan (in Parliament):
>*Where should we ever find so base a rogue?*

A Foppish Member of the House:
>*Hear! Hear!*

Sheridan (sitting down):
>*I thank you, sir,*
For your prompt information.

A reputation for malingering
    Preceded Palmer everywhere he went.
    He had refined the art of the excuse
    Which frequently involved his wife, invoked
    When sheriffs, creditors or bailiffs called.
    'My friends,' he'd say, his handkerchief produced
    And flourished most affectingly, 'my friends,
    I cannot be with you today. My wife,
    The partner of my joys and sorrows, is
    Just now confined' (a happy crisis which
    Seemed to occur at weekly intervals).
    His *Joseph Surface* was admired. Perhaps
    His *Falstaff* lacked a certain boisterousness.
    'He was a *gentleman* and yet there was
    A slight infusion of the *footman*.'

                            Once
The actor, at his home in Kentish Town
Was bitten on the eye-lid by a wasp
While nailing up a grape-vine. He sent word
His eye was closed, he could not take the stage.
And at the theatre late apologies
Were made for his indisposition.
                            Then
A gentleman rose in the pit
And stated that he was concerned that this
Was one more instance of the actor's quite
Disgraceful fraudulence. The audience
Were so incensed that nothing now would serve
But that the actor must be sent for.
                            Thus
It was that after some remonstrances
The manager himself – paint, pumps and all – set off
For Kentish Town, where he found Palmer much
In pain, not shamming, with his eye quite closed.
The manager explained the restiveness
Which fuelled the audience, and so convinced
Poor Palmer to return with him, undressed
For anything but convalescence.
                            So
In haste the two returned by coach. And when
The actor walked on to the stage, the light
And distance rendered his afflicted eye
Quite imperceptible, the audience hissed
And jeered, and cheered the gentleman in the pit.
Palmer advanced beneath a heavy fire
Of orange peel and finally was allowed
To speak. 'My lords, ladies and gentlemen,

I am aware that my appearance here
Must seem quite odd to some of you – ' Loud cries
Of 'Shame!' 'How true!' 'Well, what is wrong?'
        'The fact,
Ladies and gentlemen – let me explain –
Is this. My illness was – *all – my eye.*'

The contest of the Romeos:
 At Drury Lane shone David Garrick;
 At Covent Garden, Spranger Barry.

Opinion was divided then
Between these two. Intense debate
All day brewed in the coffee shops.

Macklin thought Barry 'swaggered so
And in the garden scene spoke up
So loudly, servants must have heard.'

Yet it was generally agreed
That Barry at the balcony,
And at the tomb, carried the day

While in the Apothecary's street
And with the Friar, Garrick's strong
And forceful passion won the palm.

The battle raged for twelve long days.
'While Garrick drew the most applause
Yet Barry drew the most tears'

For Barry's 'amorous harmony,
His melting eyes and plaintiveness'
Touched many hearts. A lady wrote,

'I thought – had I been Juliet
To Garrick's Romeo he might
Have climbed into my balcony;

But were it Barry calling me,
So tender and so eloquent,
I would have clambered down to him.'

One evening when *Pizarro* was the play,
    All expectation in the audience turned
    To restlessness when after long delays
    The curtain had not risen on the stage.
    John Kemble (Rolla) came down to the lights
        And spoke to this effect:
'Ladies and gentlemen, at the request
Of all the players in the piece tonight
But one, I am to announce that we await,
    Still, Mr Emery,
Who on this evening plays the Sentinel –'
Scarcely had Mr Kemble spoken when
In great-coat, dirty boots, his face all red
And wet with perspiration, rushed on stage
The culprit. Emery panted for some time,
Attempting to regain his breath, then spoke:
    'Ladies and gentlemen,
This is the first time I have had to speak
As an apologist. But since I am
The sole cause of delay, allow me now
To offer my excuse, when, I am sure,
I shall obtain acquittal – especially
From the fair part of this brilliant audience.
    Fair ladies,
(For you I must particularly address)

                My wife –' (And here
The speaker's feelings almost overcame
            His eloquence) 'My wife
Was but this hour since brought to bed and I – '
(Mounting applause delayed the apology)
'And I ran for the doctor – ' (More applause.
'You've said enough!' exclaimed a thousand tongues.)
'I could not leave her, ladies, until I
Was sure –' ('Well done!') 'that she was safe.' ('Bravo!'
'You've said enough!' 'Bravo!' 'Well done!')
Now Emery was overcome and bowed
And placed his hand upon his heart and bowed
Again, to every corner of the house.
The play could now begin. But in the scene
Before the prison-scene when Rolla tries
To corrupt the sentinel by bribery
An alteration happened in the lines:
    Rolla: *Have you a wife?*
    Sentinel: *I have.*
    Rolla: *Children?*
    Sentinel: *Two*
*Or, rather, I had two this morning but
    I now have three.*
Now loud applause made it impossible
For Kemble to continue in the scene.
With no sign of abatement he at length
Entered the prison without further words.

The young Miss Mellon called on Sheridan
    At his request. Miss Mellon earnestly
    Desired to join the company but seemed
    Unnerved. When Sheridan suggested that she read
    The part of Mrs Malaprop aloud

(From his own play *The Critic*) she cried out
With genuine naivety, 'Oh, Sir!
I dare not, for my life! I had rather read
To all of England. But suppose, sir – this!
Suppose, sir, you read from the play to me.
I would be honoured.' Sheridan – despite
The oddity of this arrangement – felt
The true simplicity of the request
And read almost the entire play to her
With relish. For she listened ardently
And Sheridan felt such confidence at this
He gave Miss Mellon roles in this very play.

Charles Mathews died in 1835
And so there passed a man of infinite
Variety, of 'strange inventiveness',
A man 'accomplished in the comic arts'.
This 'long thin living skewer of a man',
This 'master of disguise and mimicry'
Once entertained a party at his house.
'The last three of our guests had not arrived:
The kindly Mr Gilman and his wife,
And Coleridge who resided at that time
With them at Highgate. Snow began to fall
And doubts were entertained as it increased
Concerning Mrs Gilman's walking there.
Then Mathews played at shaking out his coat;
He paused and frowned and gave us Coleridge:
    "My dear Mr Mathews
    Such was the inveteracy of
    The angry element in its fleecy descent
    That to encounter it was barely possible
    To Mr Gilman and myself;

        For one, then, of the softer sex, the affair
        Must be impracticable."
No sooner had our laughter run its course
Than the gate bell rang, and those two gentlemen
Were shown in. Coleridge began at once:
        "My dear Mr Mathews, such was
        The inveteracy of the angry element et cetera."
And it was with some difficulty that we
Received the opinion with due seriousness.'

At Barry's funeral in the Abbey,
                Macklin, pressing close
Was turned back, by a verger, from the grave.
        Persisting, Macklin said,
'I want to see how
                he performs the part,
For soon I may be called upon
                to play the very rôle
In that same tragedy.'

Four years before his death in poverty
    The Theatre Royal reopened. Sheridan
        Had by this time learnt well the role
Of cheerfully evading creditors.

Holland, the architect, was still unpaid
And sought the elusive manager on the stage
        At a rehearsal. Sheridan
Rushed up to him and warmly shook his hand.

'Holland! The very man I wished to see –
You want a cheque? Of course. How beautiful
        Your building is, beyond reproach,
Save for a trifle – but, it must be said,

Important. Well, I see I must be frank:
My gallery customers can't hear a word.'
 'Impossible!' The architect
Was much alarmed. 'Is it? Well, you must judge.

Wait here and I'll speak from the gallery.'
So Holland stood downstage while Sheridan
 Ran upstairs to the shilling seats,
Gesticulating and apparently

Declaiming violently with open mouth
But actually not uttering a word.
 Descending to the stage, he said
'Well, Holland! Could you hear me?' 'Not a word.'

'Are you convinced? No? Well then, you go up
And you speak while I listen. We must be sure.'
 When Holland reached the gallery,
He spoke unheard, for Sheridan had gone.

Pepys:

'I went then to the theatre where I saw
Again *The Lost Lady* which do now
Please me better than before; and here,
I sitting in the dark, a lady spit
Backward upon me by mistake – she
Not seeing me, but after seeing her
To be a very pretty lady, I
Was not more troubled at it after all.'

Henry James:

'My frail little play seems already, thank God, ancient
History though I have lived through in its company
 The horridest four weeks of my entire life.

How such an ordeal – odious in its essence – is
Only made tolerable, even palatable,
    By great success while non-success may be

Tormenting and tragic, a bitterness every hour
Ramifying into every throb of consciousness.
    Tonight my poor play will be "taken off"

And will have lived the whole of its little troubled life
Of 31 performances to be replaced by
    A piece of Oscar Wilde which, probably,

Will have a very different fate. On that opening night,
Too nervous to do anything else I had the thought
    Of going to some other theatre as

A means of being coerced into a quietness
From 8 till 10.45. I went accordingly
    To the Haymarket to a new piece by

The said O.W. which was recently produced –
An Ideal Husband. I sat through it and saw it played
    With every indication of success

And that gave me the most fearful apprehension – for
The thing seemed to me so helpless, so crude, so clumsy,
    Feeble and vulgar that as I walked back

Across St James's Square to learn my own fate all this
That I had just seen seemed to constitute a dreadful
    Presumption of the wreck of *Guy Domville*

And I stopped in the middle of the Square, paralysed
By the terror of this probability – afraid
    To go on and learn more. How can my play

Succeed with a public with whom that is a success?
But if this sad episode has by this time become,
> As I said, ancient history to me

It is because when a thing for me is done, it's done.
I get quickly detached and away from it, and am
> Quite given up then to the fresher life

Of the next thing to come. This is particularly
Now the case with my literary way blocked so long
> And my production smothered by these lures

Of the theatre and its lights and representations
Of the face and human action and discourse.
> Such arrears on hand and so many things

Seem to wait for me – which I want so much to do –
That I am looking in quite another direction
> Than that of my sacrificed little play.'

Carlyle:
'I actually went one idle night
Before Jane came, to Covent Garden;
> found

It a very mystery of stupidity
And abomination and so tiresome
That I came away long before the end
And declare the dullest sermon I ever heard
Was cheery in comparison with it.'

When Barry failed as Manager
> In Dublin, and the lease was passed
> To Ryder, the forlorn affair
> Had swallowed £30,000.
> The inventory of articles

Bequeathed by transfer with the lease
Reveals a certain sad neglect:
'Chambers (with major holes in them);
House (very bad); Battlements (torn);
One stile (broken); One garden wall
(Quite bad); Woods (greatly damaged); Clouds
(Of little worth); Wings (with holes);
Wings (in bad order); Mill (torn);
Elephant (very bad); Car
Of Alexander (some wanting);
One waterfall (with damaged course)',
This sombre litany offset
By 'eighty thunder bolts (some good)',
And add to this, at Drury Lane,
When Barry played Othello – this:
A most exceptional event,
Applause from Colley Cibber, who
Was once thought never to applaud.

The treasurer at Drury Lane
    When asked to comment on the play
    (Which he had never watched), would say
        'Needs cutting.'

    He was not given to debate
    And would not add another word.
    One morning Planché called on him:
        'I asked him,

    "Mr Dunn, sir, would there be
    Objections to my sending up
    A friend to my box one night next week?"
        He looked up,

But made no answer and went on
Unfolding cheques and counting them.
I waited patiently until
> He finished.

He turned to other matters. Still
There was no answer. Finally,
Without another word, I left
> Discreetly,

And saw to other business.
Some four hours later I returned
And asked if Mr Dunn was still
> In his room.

No one had seen him leave. I went
Upstairs. I did not speak. He took
A pinch of snuff and said, "No, I
> Should think not.""

When Mr Johnson, maker of machines,
> Extravagances and automata
> At Covent Garden, went to Drury Lane
> To witness a real elephant on stage
> He seemed quite unimpressed and said, 'I should
> Be exceeding sorry if I could not make
> A more convincing elephant than that.'

A Method actress in America
> Was fond of realistic violence.
> In fact, when called upon to strike in rage,
> She'd summon up such vehemence all the cast
>> Feared injury at her hand.
> And in *The Trojan Women*, for some weeks

Talbythius already had received
A bleeding nose and several bruises from
A Cassandra set on verisimilitude
> Despite the cast's complaints.
Now at a matinee she had resolved
To quite surpass all past performances,
And fetched a massive blow. Talbythius
Felt startled blood well up in him. He cried,
> 'Guards, take her away!'
And since this was before her major scene
She struggled very realistically.

Almost a metaphor
> For the very act of speaking from the stage,
> Projecting essences
> Across a snow of candlelight
> Into the great Disorder of the Pit,
> This circumstance:

> The Burbages unable to resolve
> Disputes about their Theatre's lease
> Came therefore with their Company by night
> Dismantling, even to *the boards*,
> Its timbers which, by flare of circled moon
> And torches' frostlight in the cold,
> They took across the floating frozen Thames
> To rebuild on the further bank
> *That wondrous Polygon, that prodigious Globe.*

When Johnson came to tea
> And Garrick flew into a rage
> With prodigal Peg Woffington
> Who put too many tea-leaves in the pot,

This heaped one further straw
Upon the swaying camel's back
Of his reputed parsimony
(A reputation known to audiences).
One night the jester Weston was to play,
But sent distressing messages
To Garrick asking for a loan –
As he would often do –
Claiming to be arrested.
Garrick would not pay the debt
And so announced (as manager)
That 'Mr Weston has been taken ill
And cannot take his place.'
At this pronouncement Weston stood
And from the shilling gallery,
Held firmly by a seeming bailiff, cried,
'I'm here. I've been arrested for a debt
Which I can't pay.' The audience
Took Weston's side, demanding that
This trifling debt be paid
And Weston be allowed
To take the stage. Garrick was forced
To acquiesce and pay the debt
And welcome smiling Weston to the stage.

Seeking simplicity,
                Chekhov
Spoke highly of a school boy's copybook
And one short sentence there,
                The sea was huge.

Sandford was often said to be
    The most convincing villain on the stage.

The public would not have it otherwise,
    And they would not endure

    The slightest hint that he might hide
Integrity or decency or truth;
They trusted him implicitly to spurn
    The slur of innocence.

    An author once allotting him
(With quite regrettable naivety)
A character of lofty rectitude,
    The audience assumed

    That all these signs of piety
Would in the resolution fall away
And, at the close, be seen for what they were –
    Delicious deviousness;

    They saw in sanctity sheer guile,
And so applauded in each noble deed
The villain as dissimulator. But,
    As Act V plodded on,

    And no one yet had been betrayed,
No family fortune filched, no ruin planned,
No poisoned chalice offered by the host,
    No maiden's virtue stained,

    And Sandford triumphed in full light,
The audience rose and soundly damned the play
For its betrayal of their trust in him
    And all their fondest hopes.

A story made familiar
    By imitations or, perhaps,

An accident of echoes:
          Here,

Beaumont and Fletcher at an inn
Discuss the writing of their play;
And Fletcher says, *I'll undertake*

To kill the King, which treasonable words
An idle waiter overhears
Without awareness of their craft.

That waiter then informs on them;
Charges are brought until, in mirth,
The truth disclosed, these are dismissed.

'Miss Smithson is perhaps two creatures – one
    Who captured Berlioz in a lightning-flash,
The other strangely diffident, remote;
This may explain her mesmerising power,
Since what may seem at times ungraspable
May then seize us with even greater force…
At first she seems quite tepid, vacuous,
As if she were receding from our gaze
And were as yet unable to decide
The here and now would do and could become
Sufficiently a rock to build on; then
As soon as the effect is imminent
She starts upon an energy of voice,
Of promptitude, decision, gesture, tone.
The emery wheel is brought upon the blade;
She flings into the words its sudden flame
And then her voice, scarce audible before,
Becomes as strong and tremulous with passion

As earlier it had seemed a passing cloud.
Her eyes flash with indignant fire, the once
Sweet awkwardness of carriage now gives way
To animation which is eloquent
And filled with purpose, violently exact.
She has two voices, almost, it would seem,
Two natures balanced in a paradox
Whose excellences far outweigh the rest.
The explanation seems to us to lie
In this conjunction: to a natural art
Was overlaid an artifice, a style
Of recitation which must serve to freeze
That art below it like a darkened stream
Beneath a floor of ice – which, once her powers
Are wakened by Parisian applause,
Bears forth in flood The Present offered up
As angular and pitching as might seem
The thing itself. But then, as suddenly,
This wave may quite recede and she become
Again the fading shadow of her self…'

Macready's adjurations were in vain.
The First Murderer would persist
In walking to the centre of the stage,
Thus hiding from the audience
Macready's statuesque Macbeth. He called
A carpenter and said, 'You see
That plank there? Bring a hammer and a nail
And drive the nail into that plank.'
And it was done. 'Now, sir,' (the Murderer)
'You see that nail? Come to that spot
And not an inch beyond, and wait

Until I come to you.' The Murderer
Was most agreeable. Night came
And thus the Banquet scene. The Murderer
Entered and walked downstage and paused
And looked about and turned and stared and peered
And turned. The audience began
To puzzle with him, then to laugh at him.
Macready strode downstage and said,
                'Good Heavens, man,
What are you at?'
                The Murderer
Looked puzzled and, forgetting where he was,
Said, 'Why, I'm looking for that nail of yours.'

Miss Fanny Kemble saw in Kean
        'an eye
Like an orb,
        a voice
Exquisitely melodious
        yet
In the dissonance
        of vehement passion,
Terribly true.
        Who that ever heard
Will ever forget the tenderness,
        the anguish of
His 'Oh Desdemona, away, away!'
Who that ever saw
        will ever forget
The fascination of his dying eyes
        in *Richard*
When deprived of his sword,
        their power

Yet seeming to avert the arm
                of Richmond?
If he was irregular,
        erratic,
                    or wayward,
So is Niagara
Compared with the fountains of Versailles.'

Miss Kemble on *detachment*:
    'I have played Ophelia three times
                    with my father now,
    And each time in the affecting scene
                    where Hamlet's madness
    And his love
                    pour forth together like a stream
    In flood, a torrent swollen
                  with a gathering storm
    That bears a thousand blossoms on its troubled wave,
    I have experienced such a deep emotion as
    Would not let me speak.
                    The exquisite tenderness, the wild
    Compassion in his voice, the pity of his looks
    Ensured that scarcely had my eyes
                    been fixed on his
    They filled with tears and
                    long before the scene might end
    The letters and the jewel case I tended him
    Were wet with them.'

A tale where all is genial:
    One day (it must have been a day
    Of sunlight making clouds like hay
    Piled high in sheaves on gilded fields)

Haydn, at Reynolds' studio, found
The sitter was Mrs Billington,
The singer from the Opera
Whose singing Haydn much admired.
(How closely to sonata form
The modulating day conformed
With this benign development!)
The painting happily portrayed
This Mistress of the Ornament
(And Ornament of the Opera House)
As St Cecilia listening to
The Music of the Spheres. Haydn
Looked closely at the portrait. 'Ah!'
He said. 'While it is very fine,
The likeness unmistakable,
There is however one mistake –'
(A slight cloud hovered near the sun)
'Why, what?' cried Reynolds with a frown.
'You've painted Mrs Billington
Attentive to the angels. But
You should have represented them
As listening ardently to her.'
The subject was so very charmed
By this judicious compliment
(A grove of trees was bright in flower,
A fountain fell into its stream)
She sprang up from her pedestal
Breaking her pose, and blithely threw
Her slender arms round Haydn's neck.

Cooke being very merry at the inn,
    When Incledon came in he greeted him
        Requesting him to sing *The Storm*.

The hour was late and Incledon refused
And went to bed. But Cooke was gravely piqued
    And after musing for a time

Asked several waiters if they knew the man
Who lately sat with him. They all agreed
    It certainly was Incledon.

'Impossible!' cried Cooke. 'It has to be
Some vile impostor, for he has just now
    Stolen my watch and all my notes.

I insist an officer be sent for, that we may
Find him and search him for my property.'
    Remonstrances were all in vain,

And soon a party filed into the room
Where Incledon was sleeping. Cooke declared,
    'This imitation Incledon

Must have my watch and notes upon him. Or
If he would prove that he is Incledon
    Then let us hear him sing *The Storm*

And I will be convinced.' Now well awake
And seeing round his bed in candlelight
    His rapt expectant audience,

The one and only Incledon stood up,
Smiling at Cooke's ingenious stratagem
    And sang three verses of *The Storm*.

An art of naturalness and reticence
    Which gives the greatest pleasure on the stage
    Is noted in the following brief aside
    By Mrs Mathews in her husband's *Life*:

'In Mr Dowton's acting we might see
The fabled fountain of antiquity
Whose water, it was said, bubbled as if
To boil yet never steamed or overran
But always fell back cool upon itself.'

Before the end of Act I on
    The opening night of Mrs Griffith's
The Platonic Wife it was
Completely plain the play had failed.

So bad was it, two principals
Between the scenes thrust out their heads
From opposite wings and in a kind
Of antiphon most earnestly

Entreated all the audience
To damn the play at once and save
A painful night for everyone
Who could be happier elsewhere.

One night at Portsmouth, Barry Sullivan
    Was playing Hamlet to an audience
Almost entirely formed of sailors. At
    To be or not to be
One sailor shouted, 'Barry! If you will,
Give us a hornpipe.' Others joining in
Cried, 'Yes, but mind it is a sailors' one.'
    In mid-soliloquy
The actor was obliged to step downstage
And remonstrate with these immoderate
Demands for dancing. Then *To be*
    Or not to be resumed

Until again a voice, this time deep bass
And Herculean, interrupted, 'Are
You going to give us honest sailor folk
    The hornpipe that we want
Or am I going to have to come down there
And make you?' Sullivan was so amused
At this insistence on a dance before
    His long soliloquy
Could be completed that he smiled and turned
And, drawing on his long experience
Of acting Black-eyed Susan's William,
    Performed a hornpipe, so
Persuasively that after loud applause
He could return in expectation's hush
To take the throne chair and begin once more
    To be or not to be…

The actor Powell, a bastion
    Of imperturbability,
    Was quite indifferent
    To everything but his own lines.

Thus Elliston already drunk
And swimming through the final scene
Of *Richard III* should say
Your son, George Stanley, is he living?

But says with blurring carelessness,
Your son, George Stanley, is he dead?
Powell (as Stanley):
He is, my lord, and safe in Leicester town.

Elliston (sensing something wrong):
I mean – ah – is he missing still?

Powell (as Stanley):
He is, my lord, and safe in Leicester town.

'When Mr Morton was Examiner of Plays
    For Drury Lane, I asked for his opinion on
    Halevey's opera called *Temptation*. He replied,
    "Dear Bunn,
    By not leading you into Temptation, I
    Deliver you from evil. Truly yours, T.M."'

Addison:
    'As I was walking in the street
    I saw a fellow with a cage of birds
    And as I wondered to what use they might be put
        I heard him say they were
    Sparrows for the Opera.

    Sparrows for the Opera!
    I heard him say they were to be released
    And fly above the stage. I was still curious
        And found the sparrows' role
    Was to enact the part of birds

    Who sing in a delightful grove.
    And yet I wondered thus. Since this has been
    An opera so many times performed, with flights
        Of birds released each night
    How shall the house be rid of them?

    And might they not appear again
    In other plays in quite improper scenes
    Swooping through Ladies' chambers, or perched on a throne?
        And what of the audience,
    The mischief brought down on their heads?'

Macklin showed his comedy to Quin
    And asked his friend for an opinion. Quin
    Gave him some future hopes
    But counselled some delay in staging it.

The season passed and Macklin once again
Asked if it might not be performed. And Quin
Again urged some delay.
The following year the playwright asked again

And was astonished to receive from Quin
The same response. When Macklin showed chagrin
And asked quite peevishly
How long his play should wait to be received

The answer startled him. Unsmiling, Quin
Said, 'Until Judgement Day. For then
Would seem convenient.
Your play and you would both be damned together.'

Michael Kelly:
    'What,' said I to Bannister
    'Can be the treat that Cumberland has promised us tonight?
    Perhaps he noticed when you said
    Your favourite meal was supper, and
    Intends to favour us with several little delicacies.'

Bannister professed some doubts,
But when we came back from our walk we found him in his parlour.
As I had hoped the cloth was laid
And promising upon it stood
A large dish with a plated silver cover over it.

We sat. Our appetites were keen.
Our eyes were fixed upon these dainties soon to be revealed.
And after fussing for some time
Our host called on a servant, who
With ceremony lifted off the cover to lay bare

Another play in manuscript.
'Well. There you are my boys,' said Cumberland. 'There is the treat
I promised you. *Tiberius*,
My tragedy in five acts!
And, after we have had a little wine and water, I

Propose to read you every word.
I think I am not vain – but yet I do think it by far
The best play I have written yet,
Far better I do now believe
Than that poor comedy I read to you this yester-night.'

The threat itself was horrible
And yet the reader must believe our host was serious
And did in fact fulfil his threat
And read the first three acts to us
But seeing our fatigue proposed that we should go to bed

And leave until the morning all
The pleasures of the crises of the fourth and fifth acts.
We slept most gratefully but rose
At first light and had left before
Our host was out of bed. Such are the perils and escapes
Of travellers who would be the guests of country dramatists.

Obliging patrons are quite rare.
    A gentleman stepped lightly from the street
    And said, 'One ticket please.'

'Yes, sir. One ticket for *The Lower Depths*?'
He said, 'I don't care where it is
As long as I can see the stage.'

Obsessed with verisimilitude,
    A *Method* Long John Silver spent
    A week in search of parrots. Still
    He had not found *le perroquet juste*.
    A pet-shop owner said, 'I think
    I know the bird. Can you come back
    On Friday?' 'No,' the actor said,
    'That's when I'll be in hospital
    For the amputation of my leg.'

In amateur theatricals
    The Thorpedale players were supreme.
    Their recent triumph, *Hamlet*, won
    From family, friends and local press
    The highest praise. Soon afterwards
    The troupe went down by bus to see
    A London version of the same.
    On their return the villagers
    Were eager for a full report.
    The leading actor said, 'Not bad.
    Laurence Olivier played my part.'

The king was dead. Although the hour was late
    The gardens were still crowded. Sterne had come
    With Reynolds, Wilson, Garrick and his wife.
    They walked towards the parapet and passed
    Below the river bank where flares burned still.
    Soon Sterne began to fidget for the cold,
    Fearing the river damp, and said aloud,

'It is an eager and a nipping air.'
And Mrs Garrick tied her handkerchief
Around his neck. Then Wilson said in jest
'Roscius! Have an eye on that Cassius there.
Behold thy wife's *mouchoir*!' And Garrick smiled.
'Alas, poor Yorick! Is he not too wan
Too shivering, platonic, sensitive,
Morose, *intelligent* to take that part?
We'll add this cloak upon the handkerchief.'
The sheeting mist rose from the river's cold.
The crowds fell quiet at the braziers.
The moon threw out a cordon round its field.

When Robert Morley, in the first fine flush
    Of finding work, walked in a haze
    Of pleasure and delight, his signature
    Still glistening on his contract like a sun,
He was accosted by a beautiful
But over-painted person with dark eyes.
She sidled. 'Doing anything dear?'
'Oh yes,' the actor said, 'I'm pleased to say
I'm touring as a pirate in *Peter Pan*.'

Already in Act I a singer at the Opera
    Showed signs of excess hospitality;
    Throughout Act II the audience observed
    A waywardness of locomotion round the stage.

The interval before Act III was not wisely spent
And he could not go on. The manager
Stepped forward and addressed the audience
With a daringly imaginative apology:

Don Carlos would not reappear in Act III
'Because of faintness brought on by malaria.'
A voice called from the gallery,
'I wouldn't mind a glass or two of that myself.'

The essence every reader craves
   Is that surprising fact
   Which opens the fan one further quivering slat.

   For instance, 'Tennyson was sixty-five
   Before he first wrote for the stage.'
   Or the charming oddity

   Of this – in an otherwise
   Too solemn view of Irving's long career –
   'A can-can dancer raised her foot

   Adroitly lifting Irving's hat.
   An awkward pause ensued,
   But ended in applause when Irving smiled.'

Irving's opening nights were difficult.
   His wife who thoroughly disapproved
   Insisted on watching from her box.
   Of his problematic Romeo
   Florence wrote that night in her diary,
   'Jolly failure. Irving awfully
   Funny', a verdict echoed later
   In Gilbert's remark on Tree's Hamlet:
   'My dear fellow, I have never seen
   Anything so funny in my life.
   Yet it was not in the least vulgar.'

An all-round man, Benson was partial
    To river pleasures and the limpid oar,
    Its trench filling with light, the ruff of spray,
    The leisurely calm of leaning on the blade –
    And so at Stratford in *The Winter's Tale*
    Leontes left the theatre during all
    The lengthy revels in Bohemia,
    Slipped on a coat and flannel trousers, and
    Went rowing for an hour on Shakespeare's stream.
    Miscalculating he returned to hear
    His cue resounding loudly in the wings
    And rushed on – still in flannel trousers – rushed
    And speaking as the King of Sicily
    Announced his entry line, 'I am ashamed.'

Edward Petherbridge on Olivier:
    'There was a subtle difference
    Between rehearsals and the run-through. Then
    I saw that he had not been giving everything:

    You'd been aware of galleon,
    Of sails and rigging, all magnificent,
    But now you felt the wind filling every sail.'

Jane Welsh Carlyle to Jeannie Welsh,
    December 1843: '… It was
    The very most delightful gathering
    That ever I was at in London, our design

    To entertain Macready's children while
    The Tragic Actor was abroad
    And offer comfort to his wife. So amiable
    A purpose ended with the happiest results.

    Dickens and Forster worked until
    The perspiration poured from them and they seemed *drunk*
    With all their efforts. Dickens was
    The *finest* conjuror I ever saw

    Ending his hour-long pageant with the spectacle
    Of Christmas pudding made from flour and eggs
    And all the usual raw ingredients
    Boiled for one minute in a hat

    Then tumbled out before the astonished children, cooked
    And firm and fragrant. How we laughed
    And clapped. And then the dancing! Dickens *begged*
    Me on his knees to waltz with him.

    And then somebody noted by her watch
    And called out *twelve o'clock*. We ran
    And found our coats, still mirthful in the rush
    And Dickens and his wife took Thackeray home with them.'

When Irene Vanbrugh played the Queen,
    The cast said with a certain gleeful look
    There was a slip the Queen might make
    But would not tell her what it was.

    Then on the last night (when there were
    No further chances she could go astray)
    She asked and they agreed to tell
    What they had hoped each night to hear.

    'It's in your opening line, you see,
    Good Hamlet, cast thy nighted colour off.
    We hoped you'd say what we heard once,
    Good Hamlet, cast thy coloured nightie off.'

Two grenadiers stood guard on stage.
　(The audience were not deterred
　　　In seeing Garrick's art.)

Sometimes a cut-purse was detained
And once one villain was secured –
Tied fast to the proscenium arch
　　　And forced to watch the play.

One day a grenadier broke down
And wept at Garrick's eloquence
And ever willing to accept,
From every quarter, signs of praise
　　　Garrick gave him a crown.

A few days later, once again,
Another grenadier broke down
But Garrick was less generous
　　　For this was a comedy.

Davies relates in his *Miscellanies*:
Amidst a thousand anthems of applause,
When Mrs Oldfield came downstage to speak
The Epilogue, beginning with the line
'Methinks I hear some powder'd critic say'
An undistinguished man presumed to hiss.
She fixed her eye on him immediately
And pausing for a moment said, 'Poor creature'
Loud enough for the audience to hear,
With such a look of mingled scorn, contempt
And pity that a wave of fresh applause
Approved her conduct in this new particular.
And so this reptile sank in trembling fear.

Another Epilogue exerts its power:
    In 1896 a Rosalind
    In *As You Like It* spoke the Epilogue
    And at *If I were a woman I would kiss*
    As many of you as had beards et cetera,
    An eager voice came from the gods,
                    Me first, please, miss.

Bram Stoker tells of Gladstone at *King Lear*;
        He occupied his usual seat
           And seemed most interested – but not
Entirely happy. Afterwards he met

And complimented Ellen Terry, and
        Shook Irving's hand but voiced regrets
        At what could only be deplored –
Unpatriotic aspects of the play

In that it seemed to advocate at times
        Our taking aid from foreigners –
        And in particular the French –
In circumstances of domestic stress.

At least as patriotic were
    Those ladies overheard at interval
        At *King Lear*: 'How very different from
The family life of our dear Queen.'

When gales and heavy seas forced *Hamlet* back
        Indoors, at Elsinore,
The Hotel Marienlyst was made to serve –
The ballroom and eight hundred basket-chairs
        Arranged in circles – still
Despite the presence of Olivier

And actors all prepared to improvise
    There were some difficulties.
One ballroom door for instance was still locked
Which might have made an entrance for the Ghost.
    A porter told the cast
'That door must not be opened under any
Circumstances. In the architrave
A pair of blue tits have their nest. Disturbed
    They might desert their eggs
And you would not want that to happen – not
For anything so ephemeral as words.'

A bore was holding forth on ants
    To Mrs Patrick Campbell. She
Could not escape the detailed list
Of antly virtues. 'Ah, the ants!

How marvellously they're organised!
They have an army, don't you know –'
Here Mrs Campbell gravely said,
Wide-eyed, 'No navy, I suppose?'

George Alexander, actor-manager
    Never did manage well
Acting with Mrs Patrick Campbell. Once
    She saw him look at her –
In what should seem an amorous embrace –
    With such disdain she laughed.
At interval he sent a stern rebuke
And asked her not to laugh at him on stage.
    And from her dressing room
She sent back her reply. 'My compliments
    To Mr Alexander. Please

    Inform him that I never laugh at him
        Until I am at home.'

    When Mrs Patrick Campbell came
    To Hollywood,
    Answering a questionnaire,
    Under *Experience* she wrote,
    'Edward VII'.

In 1810 the sun arose
    To find the day already lit
    By Robert Coates, that illustrious name
    In rhinestones in the eastern sky.

    By afternoon that glow converged
    Upon the Haymarket theatre as,
    Alighting from his scallop shell –
    His horse-drawn, vast triumphal car –

    The celebrated Robert Coates,
    As Romeo, swept up the stairs
    Then strutted gloriously on the stage
    In spangled blue, full wig and hat,

    And soon expressed undying love
    By dragging Juliet by her hair
    About the grief-strewn tomb. Alas!
    The effort split his pantaloons.

    And wilder still was the applause
    When he laid down a handkerchief
    Explaining to the audience
    He must protect his splendid clothes,

Then extravagantly began
The task of dying – once – then twice –
Then three times to the fervent cries
Of *Encore* from the gallery.

Familiarity cannot cloud
The famous words of Sheridan

When Drury Lane burnt down
And opposite the blazing scene

(His fortune in its bright decline)
He sat, and drank some wine, and said,

'A man may surely be allowed
To take a glass of wine at his own fireside.'

An actor manager is left behind
By fame and fortune and the bus
Which took his company from their last failed run.

Now he is trudging in the provinces
Beside a shimmering canal,
When through a costume ruff of willow leaves

A slow, benevolent barge approaches. 'Ah!'
He cries, 'I prithee, bargeman, stay!
Wilt thou transport this noble player-king

Upon your worthy barge to London town?'
The bargeman dourly nods and soon
His passenger is seated on a load

Of horse dung fragrant in the curtained air.
They reach a lock. The gateman calls
'Declare your load.' The bargeman loudly cries,

'A pile of horse dung and an actor, squire.'
The silence of dark, floating leaves
Resumes until another glittering lock

Requires the same loud, ringing cry. 'A pile
Of horse dung and an actor.' Now
The actor-manager is so disturbed

That when against the backcloth of the bank
He sees the next lock in the wings
He stands precariously on his pile of dung

And calls down, 'Worthy bargee, do you think
Before the next gate we could speak
About the matter of the *billing* here?'

The night streamed past the window like a glove
    Drawn on perpetually and rapidly.
    Augustus Egg, Charles Dickens and their friends
    Looked from the window of the speeding train
    While Dickens hinted at his expertise
    In Twenty Questions and explained the rules.
    'One has to think of a man or woman or
    Inanimate object such as, let's say, *Egg*'
    They laughed at this but Egg said, 'Certainly
    This category would suit me very well,
    For guessing games requiring thought find me
    Mere rock and stone, a worse than senseless thing
    Who thinks of Nothing more than Anything.'

    Another train was scattering the night
    Like fallen leaves. It crossed America
    With Irving – lost in Absence, host to thoughts
    Of Nothing. So when Ellen Terry asked

What ghosts beguiled him he spoke haltingly,
As if quite puzzled, 'I was thinking how
Remarkable it is that I should be
Reputed as I am – an actor with
So little – nothing really – to commend,
Not face nor voice nor walk – how none of these
Distinguishes itself from other men...
How strange that I should be here now
Propelled towards success at such a rate
While night clouds race above a moonlit field.'

Another Nothing, this one powerful:
Salvation Nell contained the scene
Where Mrs Fiske as Nell sits on the floor
And holds her drunken lover's head
Without a word and waits for his arrest.
Ten minutes pass. Still she does not move;
And while the bar room is abuzz
With action, gradually the audience
Are watching only Mrs Fiske.
Miss Mary Garden said, 'If only we
Could manage to do *nothing* as she does.'

A graceful compliment: When Voltaire's tragedy *Alzire*
    Was first produced a rumour spread, that it was not
    The author's work. A staunch admirer said he hoped
    That this was true and, questioned further, explained himself:
    'Why, then we would have two great writers and not one.'

The woods each day rewrite the fall of leaves,
    Each day the river bank acts out an altered scene,
    Birds take up different groupings in the trees.

But when Voltaire desired to alter certain lines
In *Zara* his most recent tragedy
Dufresne, the actor, would not countenance one change

Refusing even interviews with him.
And so Voltaire resorted to the blandishments
Of Nature, in particular, partridge pie.

This succulence was made and sent anonymously.
Dufresne, who had a partiality
For partridge pie was tempted by its fragrant shell.

The pie was served. The actor was surprised
To find in each bird's mouth a copy of the lines.
Amused, replete, Dufresne relearned the part.

A footnote to Voltaire:
The manager of Drury Lane
Provided him with copies of each play
And every night he followed with the text
Until, in six or seven months,
He had learnt English perfectly.

Shelley reluctantly agreed to go
    With Peacock to the theatre. Equally
    Reluctantly he was constrained to stay
    Until the final curtain. Peacock tells
    How in *The School For Scandal*, at the point
    When, after *Surface* jollity, the scene returns
    To Joseph's library, Shelley proclaimed
    'I see the purpose of this comedy.
    We are to associate the *Virtuous*
    With bottles and glasses, *villainy* with books.'
    And after this pronouncement he desired

To leave. Quite frequently he talked about
'The withering and perverting force of comedy'
And Peacock thought he never watched another.

Another most reluctant theatre-goer
    Was Haydon: 'I had liked to read *Macbeth*
At midnight in my room when everything
Was silent and my hair stood out on end.
And so I could not at the moment when
I almost thought I heard poor Duncan groan
Put up with such a laceration as
The slamming of the box door, whispering
And rustling of women's dresses as they sat.
I jumped up in a fury and left the house.'

And Mathew Arnold too was diffident:
'The squalor of the place, the earthy smell
Of oranges, the dimness of the light,
The minor players' ineffectualness,
Together with the pained self-consciousness
Of Fanny Kemble and, outweighing this,
The harshness of Macready – all made worse
By the overwhelming problems of the play –
These altogether caused such wretchedness
During *Othello* the other night I'm sure
You would have felt it too had you been there.'

But contrariwise, John Hollingshead
    Writes in *My Lifetime*, 'In those days
When we got out at cricket we would bore
Holes through the theatre's stage-end wall
With cricket stumps, and through these holes
We sniffed the scent of footlights, all that strange

Bouquet of stage gas, orange peel,
Damp playbills and the mouldy scenery,
Which tells of plays and nothing else.
And sometimes too we heard the floating words,
The clash of swords, the echoing boards,
The shriek of heroines in shrill distress.'

Pepys:

There saw 'The Tempest' and between two acts
I went out to Mr Harris,
And got him to repeat to me
The words of the Echo while I writ them down
Having tried in the play
To have wrote them; but having done it
Without looking upon my paper,
I find I could not read the blacklead.
But now I have got the words clear,
And, in going in thither, had the pleasure
To see the actors in their several dresses,
Especially the seamen and monster,
Which were very droll: so in to the play again
But there happened one thing which vexed me,
Which is, that the orange-woman
Did come in to the pit and challenge me
For twelve oranges which she delivered
By my orders at a late play, at Night,
In order to give to some ladies in a box,
Which was wholly untrue,
But yet she swore it to be true.
But, however, I did deny it,
And did not pay her; but, for quiet,
Did buy 4s. worth of oranges
At 6d. apiece.

The actor Ernest Thesiger
    Feeling like melancholy Jacques
    Abandoned in the gloomy woods
    Of the dullest party in the world

    Said to the gentleman near him,
    'Hello. I'm Ernest. I'm an actor.'
    The gentleman answered, with a nod,
    'Hello. I'm George. I'm a king.'

The charm of the apocryphal:
    It was said Queen Elizabeth
    (One night when Shakespeare took the part
    Of Monarch) leaned out from her Box
    And dropped a Glove upon the Boards
    (As frolicksome as was her wont)
    To discombobulate the Bard
    At which he summoned to his side
    A courtier saying (metrically,
    Without a hindrance to his Sense)
    'Good Sir, take up our Sister's Glove.'

An actor walked into a pub
    Where Robert Atkins stood with friends.
    If only he could speak to him,
    The doyen of Shakespearians,
        He might just find some work.

    He wanted not to buy a drink
    So waited until Atkins' glass
    Was full, then introduced himself
    And with safe generosity
        Offered to stand a round.

'My glass is full, as you can see.
You could, however, buy me one
Of those cigars behind the bar.'
The young man could not now refuse;
    He left soon afterwards,

And Atkins' friends reproached him now
For what seemed most ungenerous.
'It's nothing of the kind,' he said.
'That was a lesson in timing, he
    Will some day thank me for.'

Beside his well-known verbal skills
    James Boswell showed a youthful flair
    For farmyard imitations. Thus
    At Covent Garden, in the pit
    With Dr Blair, young Boswell gave
    A vibrant lowing of a cow
    So splendidly the gallery cried,
    'Encore the cow! Encore the cow!'
    Then over-reaching he essayed
    More animals with less success.
    At which the doctor, drawing on
    The wisdom of his years, advised,
    'I would confine myself to cows.'

The actors' aim: to bring the audience
    Into a kind of rapt forgetfulness –
    Of all that seems, before the play begins,
    Demanding or distracting – raising them
    To rushing winds in secret upper rooms.

In this the audience is rather like
Topham Beauclerk in Rogers' *Table Talk*
Who quite forgets himself and slips into
A world of gentle reverie, removed
From purpose and responsibility.

He is expecting guests. He goes upstairs
To dress for dinner. Soon the guests arrive.
Their host does not appear. At length his man
Goes upstairs to his room and finds Beauclerk,
Instead of dressing for his friends has dressed
For bed, retired and now sleeps peacefully.

What are the actors' thoughts upon the stage?
What of the actors in *themselves*
When they declaim with passions not their own?

One way to answer might be to propose,
Beside this mystery, an anecdote
With faint or puzzling relevance
Thus mimicking that presence on the stage.
For, here too, truth is indirectly told:

When Doctor Fordyce, who was fond of wine,
Called on a lady patient he was drunk
But conscious of the fact. He took her pulse
But found he could not count the beats. He cried,
'Good God! Quite drunk' and soon excused himself.

Next day he woke considerably ashamed
And anxious to apologise. Just then
A letter came from Lady A—. 'Last night
Good sir,' she wrote, 'you properly diagnosed
My most unfortunate condition, which

>I must entreat you to keep secret – in
>Consideration of the enclosed –'
>The envelope contained one hundred pounds.

The actor on the stage; another tenuous
  Suggestion of the art:

>The Countess of Orkney, deaf and dumb,
>Was married by exchange of signs;
>Soon after her first child was born
>The nurse was startled to observe
>
>Her mistress standing by the crib,
>A large stone raised above her head,
>Her eyes fixed on the baby's face.
>(The nurse stood frozen at the spot.)
>
>She dropped the stone, not on the child
>But on the floor. Noise filled the room.
>The baby started at the sound;
>The Countess wept and laughed for joy.

'In something posited between
  Appearance and Reality,
  We are,' the actors say, 'like artisans
  Who work in fading finishes
  Or sculptors in a midday sun
  Who carve a figure out of ice.'

There is a dispute about the origins
  Of that most famous theatre anecdote:
  In *Lohengrin* the tenor waits his cue,
  The stage-hand lets the swan-boat go too soon;
  It trundles out on to the stage and leaves

Him stranded in the wings. Calmly he says,
'Does anyone know what time the next swan leaves?'
Some say that this was Lauritz Melchior,
Some Leo Slezak, while some others think
Tichatschek, the original Lohengrin.

Quin's formula for auditioning
    All would-be Hamlets: they recite
    To be or not to be
    And soon he says,
    'It's not to be, I fear. Thank you.'

Two Aerial Figures:
    The action of the air perhaps
    Suggests performance on the stage.
    Dame Sybil Thorndike once
    Noting distraction in her father's tone
    As he pronounced the blessing
    Asked him what his thoughts had been.
    'My dear,' he said, 'I was
    Imagining how wonderful it would be
    To swing across the aisle on a trapeze.

    And when Toscanini at rehearsal sought
    A certain nuance in *La Mer* he took
    A handkerchief of silk and let it fall
    And, as it settled, said, 'There. Play like that.'

When Lamb heard Wordsworth boast,
    'If I had a mind to, I could write
    Like Shakespeare',
                Lamb said, 'Ah!
So it's only the mind that's lacking then?'

Hogarth and Garrick at an inn
   Lamented mutually the lack
   Of likenesses of Fielding. 'Wait –

   I think,' said Garrick, 'I could make
   His face. Is this not Fielding?' 'Hold,
   For Heaven's sake,' cried Hogarth, 'Hold!

   Remain just as you are,' and sketched
   The outlines which became at length
   The gazing author of *Tom Jones*.

Wycherley being at Tunbridge for his health
   Was walking with his friend (one Fairbeard) when
   They overheard outside a bookseller's shop
   A noble, rich and beautiful, young widow,
   The Countess of Drogheda asking for
   The Plain Dealer. 'Madam,' Fairbeard said,
   'You seek the Plain Dealer. Here he is'
   Advancing Wycherley towards her. 'Yes,'
   Said Wycherley, 'This lady well can bear
   Plain dealing, for her qualities must make
   What would be compliments to others seem
   Plain dealing when addressed to her.' She smiled
   And said, 'Indeed, Sir, I am not without
   My faults, and yet I do love plain dealing.'
   'Then Madam,' Mr Fairbeard said, 'it seems
   That you and the Plain Dealer are designed
   By Heaven for each other.' And, in short,
   The two conversed, and Wycherley then walked
   With the Countess, visited her home
   And afterwards in London in a little time
   A marriage was arranged between these two.

The French dramatic author, Barthe,
    Was noted for his selfishness.
    He visited a friend to seek
    Reactions to his comedy

    But found that friend upon his bed,
    Attended by his family,
    As he approached his final hour.
    'Dear friend,' he said to Barthe, 'I am,

    As you can see now, fading fast.
    The doctors say I have at most
    An hour to live.' 'And yet,' said Barthe,
    'My comedy needs but half an hour.'

The long, slow canon of the poppies opening,
    The descant of the breaking wave delaying still

    Suggest the statue's silence in *The Winter's Tale*,
    The pauses Garrick made – which some thought overlong,
    The dappled shadows separating Pinter's words,
    The wait for Godot, and the efflorescent wait
    For Hedda's off-stage pistol shot. In these we watch

    The descant of the breaking wave delaying still,
    The long, slow canon of the poppies opening.

    A short play on the following
    Would seem a pleasing prospect. It
    Might even be a play in which
    Nothing happens – *several times*:

    Gibbon took very little exercise.
    He had been staying for some time
    With Sheffield at his country seat. And when

>At last he was about to leave
>The servants could not find his hat. 'Bless me,'
>Said Gibbon, 'I left it in the hall
>On my arrival here.' He had not stirred
>Outside the house at all in all that time.

Leigh Hunt in admiration and regret:
>If ever woman was ingenious enough
>To be effectively while never actually
>Naked, such a woman was Mrs Jordan
>By virtue of *transparency*
>Which makes the actress radiant.
>Tears of pleasure and regret
>Accompany the memory
>Of her who so personified
>Whatever shone with happiness
>In those days of our youth
>Now gone like her.

Leigh Hunt, *The Examiner*, 1815:
>Liston has often held an audience
>For five minutes at least without a word
>As in the afterpiece *The Turnpike Gate*:
>He comes in to an inn and sees at once
>A pot of ale upon a table. Then
>He looks about him with a ludicrous
>Exaggerated caution as he stares
>Then makes advances, then, half simpering
>When he is close to it, retreats again.
>He looks about with caution and draws near
>Only to hover once more turned away
>Then, heaving a sudden look into it, says

With an affected, rapt indifference,
'Oh dear. Some gentleman has left his ale.'

Pepys:
2 November 1667
To the King's playhouse and there did see
Henry the Fourth and, contrary
To expectation, was most pleased
In Cartright's speaking Falstaff's speech
On *What is honour?* and this scene.
The house full of parliament-men
It being holiday with them,
It was observable then how
A gentleman in a nearby row
Did eat of fruit throughout the play
And so did drop down as one dead
Quite choking, stifled and unwell.
But with ado came Orange Nell,
Did thrust her finger down his throat
And bring him back to life again.

Dear Sir, I wish you every joy
On the great success of your new Comedy
She Stoops to Conquer or The Mistakes of a Night.
The English Nation was about to fall
Into a lethargy. Their blood
Was thickened and their minds
Creamed and mantled like a standing Pool.
No wonder – when their Comedies which should
Enliven them like sparkling, old champagne
Were quite become mere syrup of the poppy's
Gentle soporifick draughts.
And had there been no end to this

Our Audiences must have gone
To Theatres with their night caps. While, abroad,
The Opera Houses' Boxes are set up
For drinking tea, at Drury Lane
They must have soon been furnished with settees
Commodiously arranged for sleep.
But you have waked the spirit of our mirth
Which had so long layn dormant, and revived
Our natural humour and our hearty laughter.

    You must know that my wife
Was happily delivered of a daughter, on
The very evening that *She Stoops to Conquer*
First appeared. I relish the coincidence.
My little daughter is a fine and lively child
And shall, I trust, be blest
With all the cheerfulness of your own Comic Muse.
She has none of the wretched whining ways
Which children have so often, nothing of
The recent tendency
To *comédie larmoyant*, the lachrymose,
Which you so rightly have deplored.
I hope that she will live to be
An agreeable companion and diffuse
Her gayety upon her father's days
Which have had some propensity to cloud.

    I hope to be in London in the spring
And thus to share your social hours. Meantime
I beg to hear from you.
While you are in the full refulgence of
Theatrical Splendour, while the great and gay
In London hang upon your smiles,
I hope that you can *stoop to write* to me.

>   I ever am, Dear Sir,
>   Your most affectionate humble servant,
>   James Boswell.

Dear Sir, I thank you for your kind remembrance
>   And for your letter and your congratulations.
>   I always said success upon the stage
>   Was great cry and little wool.*
>   And it gives me pleasure to hear
>   That you have increased your family.
>   I have no doubt the little stranger will
>   One day or other as you hint
>   Become a CONQUEROR.
>   Three days ago I was most horribly abused
>   By writers in the press. So like a fool
>   I went and thrashed the Editor.
>   And he is to take the law of me –
>   But come to town and we shall laugh it off.
>   I am, dear Sir, your most affectionate
>   And humble servant,
>   Oliver Goldsmith.
>   *An ancient saying thus explained
>   By Erasmus in *Adagia*,
>   Meaning 'much labour for a small reward':
>   '*Great cry and little wool,
>   The devil cried as he sheared the hogs.*'

When Elliston was manager, the harlequin
>   In jumping through a window fell with violence
>   On the other side of the scene, because the carpenter
>   Had quite neglected to position wadding there.

Unhurt but shaken he abused the carpenter
Until his shouts rang through the house. Then Elliston
Appeared behind the backdrop to investigate
And to observe, 'There was much cry and little wool'.

As Bannister stood one night unobserved
    Behind the scenes he heard
    The stage-hands arguing
    The merits of the Hamlets they had seen.

    One favoured Henderson, another Kean,
    Another Kemble. One
    Said, 'Bannister for me.
    He's twenty minutes faster than the rest.'

The beauty of Sophia Baddeley
    Was long acknowledged by the populace
    And was in popular opinion held to be
        A wonder of the age.

    When Foote, in 1771, produced
    His comedy *The Maid of Bath* (a play
    Based loosely on the long romance of Sheridan
        With the beautiful Miss Linley),

    And Mrs Baddeley was in the box
    Close to the stage, Foote said, in character,
    Descanting on the heroine's charms, 'Not even those
        Great beauties of the Muses –'

    And then interpolated, looking up,
    '– Nor those of Mrs Baddeley, divine,
    Yet with us here tonight – could exceed the Maid of Bath…'
        At this extravagance,

Applause rang through the house. Foote was encored
And called upon to say these lines again;
Affecting some confusion, Mrs Baddeley
    Rose in her box, and stood,

And so remained for several minutes, blushing
And smiling and acknowledging the roar
Of admiration and great nationalist pride,
    Upstaging all the stage.

Two days before *The Critic*'s opening night
    The last act was not finished.
                    Dr Ford
And Mr Linley, joint proprietor
At Drury Lane
        Were fidgety,
And King who was stage manager
As well as acting in the play
                resolved to grasp
The nettle. So
A night rehearsal of the piece was called
And Sheridan
          who having dined
With Linley (who was his brother-in-law)
Was thus prevailed upon to come.
                On stage
King whispered that he had
                something particular
To communicate and begged that he would step
Into the greenroom.
          There
Sheridan found a pleasant fire,

And armchair and a table,
       pens and ink
And paper and, besides,
       two flasks of claret and
A dish of best anchovy sandwiches.
King left the room and locked the door.
Linley and Ford came up
       and said to Sheridan
That until he had finished his – their – play
He would not be released.
       The author laughed
At their contrivances
       and set to work
And soon had finished
The wine, the sandwiches and, last, the play.

The actors too are sometimes as convinced
 By power and rhetoric as the audience
 And slip into the quicksand of belief
 Forgetting everything is artifice:

 When Garrick said, 'There's blood upon thy face',
 He so disturbed the First Murderer
 The man put up his hand to feel his face
 Forgetting everything to cry, 'Is there, by God!'

Dibdin's *History of the Stage*:

 'That Garrick reached perfection, insofar
 As it is in the power of humans to be perfect,
 Nothing can controvert;
 Nature had given him
 A most intelligent and comprehensive mind,
 He knew the passions and their subtle shades,

Distinctions and gradations, to infinity,
He knew the manner of their utterance;
And all his author meant
And all expressed, he knew.
So, let the thought be ever so illustrious,
It still came mended from his rendering of it.

So great was his command over his form
And features that the imitative boundaries
From kingly dignity
To drivelling idiotism,
Were all at his command. But it is enough to say,
Although his fame needs no eulogium,

He did not leer at ladies near the stage,
He contemplated no appointments to be kept
With pleasure after the play,
He planned no panegyric
In his favour for the next morning's papers.
In fact I shall content myself to tell

What he was not: in his utterance
He was not ever tedious, monotonous,
Precise or unimpassioned,
Cold or indistinct;
Nor did he bellow, flounder, splutter, whoop or rant.
In his deportment he was not affected,

Lounging, languid, awkward; nor did he
Once shuffle, stalk or stride or kick. He neither shook
His head like a panteen
Nor buffeted the air
With flailing arms, nor fluttered like a butterfly
Or rolled about like porpoises at play…

In short, he never once inflated tragedy
Into a bombast, nor
Degraded comedy into buffoonery.'

The actor Bartley was reliable,
  Content to wait for roles thought suitable
  To his dependable but modest skills.

  Fawcett as Covent Garden manager
  Would use his power to take choice minor parts,
  But one day sent for Bartley. 'George,' he said,

  'I'm giving you a chance. The play next week
  Is *Hamlet* and I think I can entrust
  The First Gravedigger to your proven powers.'

  Delighted, Bartley expressed his gratitude
  While wondering Fawcett did not want the role.
  And Fawcett shook his hand and wished him well.

  But later Bartley overheard him say,
  'These winter nights the wind that comes up through
  The grave-trap is enough to freeze the blood.'

For all the charms of nature, plied and pied,
  The smell of grass and cows and dust, the breeze,
    The stage-front set with bales of hay
  And garlanded with flowers still in bud,

  The play *The Stage Coach* was so badly done
  The audience was confused. A local squire
    Sought out the manager and asked
  What was the entertainment they had seen.

'Why, it's *The Stage Coach*,' said the manager.
'Then would you be so good to let me know
      When it is to be played again
That I might be an outside passenger.'

An eighteenth century *bon-mot*:
    The author of some wretched tragedies
    Was asked why he did not attempt
    A comedy.
               'Because,' he said, 'I fear
    That after reading Molière,
    I have not the temerity.'
                    The other mused,
    'A pity that you did not read Racine.'

A stratagem designed to clear the room
    Of would-be playwrights, dread monologists,
    Bombastic bores and readers-of-their-plays,
    Hawkers of fustian, ancient mariners,
    Purveyors of loquacity who just,
    By good chance, happen to be carrying
    A five-act tragedy about their persons:

A manager at Covent Garden was
Importuned by an Irish curate who,
Prevailing on his patience, offered him
Five tragedies and five droll comedies
All in his hand, the ink scarce dry, and said,
He would read just one of each (so as to save
Much precious time for both of them) and chose
Lord Russell from his store of tragedies
And *Draw the Long Bow* from the comedies
And breathlessly began. The manager,

Politely patient, listened in much pain
Resolving to despatch him permanently.
He waited till the fourth act, then he said
'It's very fine indeed, quite excellent.
But don't you think your hero should by now
At least have made his entrance?' 'Hero, Sir!
What hero?' 'Why, your character Lord Russell
Has not been on yet.' 'What! Lord Russell, Sir?
I have been reading from the comedy
Of *Draw the Long Bow*,' and with much hauteur,
Disdain and glaring rage he gathered up
His nine more manuscripts and left in haste.

Though Jedediah Buxton could not write
   He was the calculator of the century.
   In 1754
   He walked to London to see royalty,
   This being his only interest other than
   The milky way of numbers.
   At this time he entertained
   A crowded meeting of the Academy
   By cubing numbers of a hundred digits.
   He said that he was *drunk* once from the feat
   Of reckoning by memory for a month –
   But slept for seven hours and recovered.
   He married and had several children who
   Exhibited nothing of this faculty.
   In London he was taken to the theatre
   Where Garrick took the role of Richard III.
   He was unmoved
   By all the splendours of the stage
   Or by the actors' eloquence

>But told the number afterwards
>Of words he'd heard
>And steps the dancers took
>And ratio of speech to silences.

The history of performance could be seen
>As aspects of a tournament – or at times
>Pitched battle – with the combatants
>The actor and the author.
>Thus Kemble playing Hamlet in the provinces
>Was startled by his Guildenstern.
>For at the lines
>When Hamlet asks him, 'Will you play
>Upon this pipe?' and he replies,
>'My lord, I cannot,'
>This Guildenstern was eager to display
>His musical abilities
>And said instead,
>'Well, if my lord insists
>I'll do as well as I can do,'
>And turned downstage and played God Save the King.

The consequences of caprice
>Or vanity or just thickheadedness
>In actors by their rendering –
>Or rending – may, for their authors, be
>More painful than is generally allowed.
>One day *Tartuffe* was on the stage.
>A gentleman spoke to Molière in the wings,
>When suddenly the latter cried,
>'That dog! That burglar! O that butchering wretch!'
>And struck his fist against his head.
>The gentleman was startled and mistook

This frenzy for a seizure or a fit.
Then Molière, recovering, said,
'Sir, it was only this – an actor who
Spoke seven of my lines most shamefully
Without accent or gesture. And to see
My children so molested in this way
Torments me like a soul condemned.'

A curious instance of
The theatre as medicinal,
Restorative or balm:

An ailing player who refused
To take all medicines
Obliged his doctor to devise

Some way to make him take the draught.
The play contained a scene
In which, as sentenced prisoner,

The hero is obliged to drain
A poisoned cup of wine;
The actor, in this character,

Discovered as he raised the cup
Port wine had been replaced
By senna. Ah, how brilliantly,

How painfully he played this scene!
With what reluctant sighs
He loathed yet drank the dreadful cup –

So he excelled himself;
As he threw down the empty cup
The applause was deafening.

At 70 Paul Léautaud
    Abandoned criticism and the theatre.

    His ego had become so great, some said,
    That to be forced to sit for several hours

    In silence while the actors spoke aloud
    Became at last intolerable.

The art of the lugubrious
    By which the emptiness of words –
    Words which like sieves let meaning drain from them –
    Is well attested,
                   shone in the comic skills
    Of Perlet of the *Comédie-française*.
    Gloomy, taciturn,
                   his was the comedy of one
    Long-suffering and suffering silently.
    And yet his misanthropic eye
    Was lightened by the daughter of
    Tiercelin, an equally morose
    Comedian of silences.
                   An interview
    Was organised by mutual friends. The two
    Sat down alone to dinner. By dessert
    Neither had spoken, not a single glass
    Was plunged into the oak-aged vintage cask
    Of meaning.
                   At the banquet's end
    Tiercelin refolded and replaced
    His napkin, rose and took the other's hand
    And looked about him with a mournful air
    And said, 'You're just the son-in-law I want.'

The stalls were like a field of empty graves.
    The actress spoke in hushed, confiding tones.

    'My dear,' her lover said, 'you may speak out.
    There's no one there tonight to hear our plans.'

A failed experiment: on holiday
    In Manchester Jack Bannister sought out
    A manager and asked to be allowed
    To play some small role in a comedy

    Under another name, and afterwards
    To attempt (between the play and after-farce)
    To imitate 'a scintillating scene
    From *The Children in the Wood*, exactly as

    Portrayed by the much esteemed Jack Bannister
    Of London's Theatre Royal at Drury Lane.'
    The manager agreed. The comedy
    Was well received, the Waiter much admired.

    But in *The Children in the Wood* a mood
    Of disapproval soon gave rise to scorn
    And hisses at the attempt to imitate
    The inimitable, unique Jack Bannister.

The ideal actor must be versatile,
    Responsive to nuance of character
    But, equally, to unexpected holes
    Which may break through the fabric of the piece –
    Flaws to be hidden from the audience.

    The play was one of many (popular
    At the time) in which sea battles shook the stage

As ships contended in a turbulent swell
Which fifty stage-hands made with canvas waves.

While Fechter played a pirate on his brig
Engaging with two proudly riding sloops
The whole engagement seemed to undulate,
The billowing canvas bright with painted foam.

Then as the enemies prepared to board
One stage-hand losing balance pushed his head
Right through the canvas ocean and appeared
Bewildered, in the centre of the sea.

But Fechter showed resourcefulness
And leaning from his brig shouted at once,
'Man overboard!' and ordered crew
To haul the startled mariner aboard.
This detail, seen as added realism,
Won from the crowd a wave of fresh applause.

Ellen Terry wore
    Her hair in deep red plaits, which fell
    From under a purple veil above a robe
    Of green on which the iridescent wings
    Of beetles glittered like an evening sky,
    And from her shoulder swept a cloak
    Embroidered in spun gold.
    Oscar Wilde remarked:
    'Judging from the banquet,
    Lady Macbeth appears
    Both economical
    And loyal to local industries
    In purchasing her husband's clothes

    And all the servants' liveries.
    But for herself she takes great care
    To do all her own shopping
    In Byzantium.'

The imperious Mrs Potter (said to be
    'A kind of minor touring Mrs Pat')

    Was noted for one further stratagem
    In the players' ancient contest with the author.

    As Mary Queen of Scots, she'd turn upstage
    And whisper to her serving girl or maid,

    'Oh, say my next line for me will you dear.
    I've never liked it from the very start.'

Frederic Lemaitre, the superb,
    Was universally admired
    Because, as it was later said,
    Of some innate vulgarity
    Which coupled with his recklessness
    Led him to dangerous extremes.

    Once he declared he would remove
    His wig while on the stage. He did.
    Success emboldened him. He next
    Announced that he would do the same
    But wipe his forehead with the wig.
    Again this was not censured. Then,

    Fired by such magnanimity,
    Swimming in freedom on the stage,
    He now essayed to take his wig
    And use it as a handkerchief.

He felt a quite delicious calm
And strode about before the storm.

The storm soon broke. The audience
Demanded an apology
Which he refused. The consequence
Was quintessentially French. For this
Offence against good taste he was
Confined for forty days in gaol.

Flamboyantly subversive on the stage
    Frederic Lemaitre in a comedy
  Was meant to drink a bottle of champagne.

  As an economy the management
  Would substitute some seltzer water. But
  One night Lemaitre stopped the play and called

  In ringing tones, 'Send for the manager!
  I want to speak to him.' The audience
  Were restless and intrigued. 'Come forward, sir!

  What do you mean by this untimely hoax!
  Am I to be made party to deceit
  And forced to be an accomplice in your scheme

  To treat the public with contempt.' 'I, sir?'
  'Yes, you, sir, you!' Then, turning to the pit
  He pointed to the manager with scorn

  And said, 'Ladies and gentlemen, you think
  That I am drinking champagne in this scene.
  But it is nothing of the kind. It is

Mere seltzer water! Yet the audience —
All you good citizens — are asked — with me —
To swallow here a palpable untruth.'

Amused by this most serious impudence
The audience cheered. The manager exclaimed,
'It is a mistake, monsieur, a mere mistake,

Upon my honour. You shall have champagne.'
And hastened off to right this grievous wrong.
Meanwhile Lemaitre waited on the stage

Discoursing nonchalantly on the theme
Of seltzer water, champagne and truth in art,
And the want of honesty in managers.

When Doctor Johnson in his carriage passed,
    One rainy day, a woman carrying
    A baby, both exposed to driving rain,
    He stopped the coach and offered her the seat
    Beside him. As she thanked him and the coach
    Set off again he warned her gravely: 'Madam,
    I wish to make it clear that, should this child,
    Responding to the motion of the coach,
    Wake suddenly, then if you should indulge
    In *baby talk* of any kind you must
    At once step from this coach.' The rain increased.
    The baby woke. The mother quite forgot
    These cautionary words and said, 'The little dear!
    Oh, is he going to open his eyesey pysey?'
    'Stop the coach,' cried Johnson. Stepping down,
    Mother and child walked on once more in rain.

Before the opening of his play
  (*Le Candidat*, which managed four
  Performances) Flaubert displayed,
  In letters to his niece, his famed
  Detachment; he is unconcerned
  About the staging of his play;
  He could not be less troubled by
  The changes the producer wants,
  For, after all, *Le Candidat*
  Is something he has finished with.
  It is no longer his. He is
  Therefore completely calm, and so
  Nothing about the play could now
  Disturb him. Then he says, 'But how
  Exasperating is the way
  So many people want free seats.'

When Harriet Smithson dazzled Berlioz
  By her Ophelia, drowning in a stream
  Of English syllables – opaque to him –
  'He swooned rather than slept' in snow-filled fields,
  Or sojourned on the frozen banks of the Seine;
  And once, at a marble table under trees
  Outside the Café du Cardinal, he sat
  Without apparent movement for five hours,
  Alarming all the waiters who (it was said)
  Dared not approach him lest they find a corpse.

An incident with thunder-balls:
  Edinburgh, 1825.
  Act III of *Lear*; a storm: behind
  The scene, a corrugated floor

On which the carpenter must wheel
A cart of nine-pound cannonballs.

He trips and falls, and tips the cart,
From which the cannonballs roll out
And, hastening down the stage incline,
Burst through the scene. The King must leap
Out of their path. They gather speed
And crash into the orchestra.

Musicians with their instruments
Were forced to climb the fence between
The orchestra and the pit, where soon
The audience sheltered from the storm.
Upstage through breached Armada sails
They saw the carpenter still lie

Beneath his upturned cart – while Lear,
Abandoning all solemnity,
Came downstage to observe the storm
Pass out of view and then subside.
The tempest past, the audience
Felt sudden pastoral merriment.

On Christmas eve in 1814, when
The Stranger was the play (a benefit
For Kemble) Mrs Cruse appeared
Much agitated.
              This was taken as
The pathos of her character
And drew forth much applause.
                      However
When the bell rang for Act V

The audience were told that Mrs Cruse
Was seriously indisposed. Her character
Would be played by another.
                            After the play
It was announced that Mrs Cruse
Had been delivered of a child.
                            The night before
She had played Juliet.
This fragment from the history of the stage
Suggests as a companion piece
Another drawn from that same time:
                            An unnamed actress
Also cast as Juliet
And recently a mother, tried to leave
Her baby in the greenroom.
                            But
Just as the balcony scene was called,
He cried so loudly she resolved
Her only course must be to play the scene
With the baby at her breast.
                            Immediately
The child was calmed, invisible
Beneath a lace shawl and obscured
Behind the balcony rail.
                            Thus she appeared,
Her other arm raised pensively,
Naively, charmingly, to her cheek.
                            The audience
Were stirred by her grave innocence.
But, alas, the play requires that Juliet
Appear and disappear three times,
And, in her effort to return and lean again

Towards her lover but not show
The nursling child, she stumbled at
The railing of the balcony
                        Which slowly fell
Revealing Juliet as a love dazed girl
Holding a baby at her breast.
                  Whereas
The applause for Mrs Cruse
Had celebrated disbelief
Suspended with enthusiasm,
                  that
For this ambiguous Juliet sprang
From startlement at its return.

When Woodward was the manager
    At Crow Street Theatre, Dublin, mobs beset
    The Parliament in order to prevent
    A hated bill.

    Some senators were held near Woodward's door
    Beside the Parliament
    And several of the mob called out
    For Woodward to throw down

    A bible so that all those senators
    Could be required to swear
    They would oppose the bill.
    But Mrs Woodward called down in alarm

    The house did not possess a Bible. 'But,'
    She cried, 'I have here in my hand
    The works of Shakespeare. Could you swear on that?'
    And threw it down.

The rabble seized the folio
As Woodward at the window with his wife
Called down, 'Yes. Let them swear on that.
It has much more validity.'

Voltaire's *Nanine*, a comedy
   Derived from Richardson's *Pamela,*

   Although successful was disliked
   By Piron, who informed Voltaire.

   Voltaire was sceptical. 'If so,
   Why then did you not hiss my play?'

   Piron replied, 'A man cannot
   Both hiss and, with the same breath, yawn.'

An actor-manager in the provinces
   For several nights appeared with Kean.

   On alternating nights the two exchanged
   The roles of Iago and the Moor

   Until one evening after too much wine
   A curious incident occurred:

   The vine had spread its tendrils through their veins
   And yet they kept the play afloat

   Nudging its way down locks and rapids, still
   Avoiding capsize and, to all

   Appearances, well manned. Kean played Othello,
   Bass the devil with forked tongue.

But reaching *Villain, be sure thou prove* –, the vine
Burst into flower. Staggering, Kean

Half grappling with Iago brought them both
Down in confusion in midstream.

Then Kean, instead of letting Bass reply
'Is it come to this?' said this himself

And Bass, taking that cue, proceeded as
Othello. Kean had now become

Iago for the remainder of Act III.
The audience, puzzled then amused,

Laughed strangely where they once were grave. Kean glared.
But anger served to clear his head.

And when at interval he caught a glimpse
Of his darkened face he cried aloud,

'By heavens, Bass, I should be the Moor tonight.'
'Of course,' said Bass. 'Then why on earth,'

Kean scowled, 'did you assume my character –'
Then both laughed at that eddying.

To overcome their strange reversal – and
The unease of the audience

Kean made the final acts a tour de force
Of mystery, power and clarity.

Peg Woffington leaves the stage for the last time:
'She was then at Covent Garden in the spring.
She had made Rosalind her own for ten years

When on the 3rd of May 1757
She wore the bridal dress. She felt strangely dazed.
A feeling of prophetic ill came upon
This vital creature as the last act began,
And yet the audience might have taken her
To be as radiant in health as she seemed.
She began the pretty, saucy prologue
With her old saucy prettiness of manner
But when she had said, "If I were among you
I would kiss as many of you as had beards
That pleased me," she paused trying to speak but was
Unable, knew that she was stricken, and gave
A wild shriek as she turned towards the stage door.
On her way she fell down paralysed into
The arms of sympathising comrades who bore
Her from the stage to which she never returned.'

Planché:

Of the eccentric and endearing
Mr Sheridan Knowles:
When I was manager at Covent Garden
One of our operas
Told of the love of a young count
For a gypsy girl whom he deserts
For a lady of rank and fortune.
In the second act
There was a fete in the chateau gardens
Honouring the bride to be.
Mr Binge, who played the count,
Was seated in an arbour near the wings
To watch a ballet. Knowles,
Who had been in the audience,

Now passed me in the wings
And coming up as close as possible
To Binge without being seen,
He whispered loudly, 'Binge!'
Binge looked across and whispered,
'Well, what is it?'
'Tell me. Do you marry
The poor gipsy girl after all?'
'Yes,' answered Binge impatiently,
And reached his arm behind him
Directing Knowles to keep back.
Knowles caught his hand and pressed it fervently
And said, 'God bless you, Binge.
You are a good fellow.'

A gracious compliment:
> The niece and former mistress of Voltaire,
>
> > Madame Denis,
>
> Was complimented on her playing of Zaïre
> At Ferney in her uncle's theatre.
>
> > 'But, alas!' she said,
>
> 'To play the part well one must be both
>
> > young and pretty.'
>
> The compliment was prompt:
> 'Ah Madame,
>
> > you are a complete proof of the contrary.'

John Drew, meticulous and elegant,
> Shaved his moustache to act in *Rosemary*.
> This altered him dramatically.

> Soon afterwards he met Max Beerbohm – but
> Could not recall his name. Max Beerbohm said,

'Well, Mr Drew, I fear you don't
Remember me without your moustache.'

Charles Laughton was – with other friends –
    A guest of Artur Rubinstein,
    Who screened for them home movies of
    His children in a play. These went on rather long.
    Charles Laughton then remarked, 'At times
    I very much regret the fact
    I have no children of my own –
    They could have entertained you with their piano playing.'

As A.E. Housman lay in death's great light,
    His doctor, knowing his taste for risqué jokes,
    Told him this:

An actor, asked how actors spend their time,
Replied, 'Sometimes we lie on the sands
           and look at the stars;
Sometimes we lie on the stars
           and look at the sands.'
'Good –' (Housman smiled) 'I – may –
        repeat – that on – The Golden Floor.'

Wilfred Worsnop Lawson,
    Actor of eccentric roles
    Met Richard Burton in the pub
    Before a matinee.

    Not due to make an entrance
    Until late in the opening scenes
    He sat with Burton in the stalls.
    Some twenty minutes later,

Burton was surprised
When Lawson tapped his arm and said,
'You'll like this bit. It's very good.
It's where I come on.'

Afterword

The idea of retelling theatre stories began with a second-hand copy of Donald Sinden's *Theatrical Anecdotes*. Other anthologies, biographies and histories followed. Widening circles of bibliographies soon spread out into earlier anthologies and accounts, from practitioners within the theatre – Oxberry, Bunn, Wilkinson, Macready – as well as from the memoirs of ardent theatregoers – Pepys, Hunt, Moore, Haydon… But the remarkable degree to which certain stories are repeated again and again makes specific acknowledgment of sources impossible. For example, Macklin's final octogenarian appearance as Shylock, Barrymore's hurling of a fish from the stage, Charles Kemble's treatment of a crying child in the audience, Garrick's parsimony, Ralph Richardson's parrot, Barry's and Garrick's competing Romeos – these are typical of hundreds of set pieces which recur almost obsessively. And the same blunder or witticism may well be attributed to a surprisingly large cast.

Perhaps the peculiar transience of everything in the theatre makes the desire to recall and record particularly keen; certainly the theatrical seems an especially vivid category of anecdote, and from general collections of them the theatrical examples often seem among the best.

As a final disclaimer, let a few words from the preface to Jacob Larwood, *Theatrical Anecdotes*, accompany this miscellany:

> It has been observed that in books of theatrical anecdotes there is probably more unscrupulousness and falsehood to be found than in any other miscellanies. On the other

hand, it may be safely concluded that very few stories, however absurd, relative to plays and players, are to be pronounced absolutely incredible. They may have been a little rouged or burnt-corked *secundum artem*, but what of that?

www.ingramcontent.com/pod-product-compliance
Lightning Source LLC
Chambersburg PA
CBHW070912080526
44589CB00013B/1270